Math Riddles For Smart Kids

Over 400 Challenging Math Riddles, Trick Questions And Brain Teasers That Kids And Family Will Love To Solve

Miranda Stewart

Math Riddles for Smart Kids

© Copyright 2020 - All rights reserved.

The content contained within this book may not be reproduced, duplicated or transmitted without direct written permission from the author or the publisher. Under no circumstances will any blame or legal responsibility be held against the publisher, or author, for any damages, reparation, or monetary loss due to the information contained within this book. Either directly or indirectly.

Legal Notice: This book is copyright protected. This book is only for personal use. You cannot amend, distribute, sell, use, quote or paraphrase any part, or the content within this book, without the consent of the author or publisher.

Disclaimer Notice: Please note the information contained within this document is for educational and entertainment purposes only. All effort has been executed to present accurate, up to date, and reliable, complete information. No warranties of any kind are declared or implied. Readers acknowledge that the author is not engaging in the rendering of legal, financial, medical or professional advice. The content within this book has been derived from various sources. Please consult a licensed professional before attempting any techniques outlined in this book. By reading this document, the reader agrees that under no circumstances is the author responsible for any losses, direct or indirect, which are incurred as a result of the use of information contained within this document, including, but not limited to, — errors, omissions, or inaccuracies.

TABLE OF CONTENTS

INTRODUCTION	5
CHAPTER 1 SIMPLE MATH RIDDLES	7
CHAPTER 2 EASY MATH RIDDLES	11
CHAPTER 3 INTERMEDIATE MATH RIDDLES	20
CHAPTER 4 MODERATE MATH RIDDLES	28
CHAPTER 5 MEDIUM RIDDLES	36
CHAPTER 6 HARD LEVEL RIDDLES	42
CHAPTER 7 CHALLENGING MATH RIDDLES	50
CHAPTER 8 FOR FUN	57
CHAPTER 9 MORE MATH RIDDLES	65
CHAPTER 10 BONUS RIDDLE	75
CHAPTER 11 SIMPLE MATH RIDDLES ANSWERS	83
CHAPTER 12 EASY MATH RIDDLES ANSWERS	85
CHAPTER 13 INTERMEDIATE RIDDLES ANSWERS	89
CHAPTER 14 MODERATE MATH RIDDLES	94
CHAPTER 15 MEDIUM RIDDLES ANSWERS	100
CHAPTER 16 HARD LEVEL RIDDLES ANSWERS	103

CHAPTER 17 CHALLENGING MATH RIDDLES ANSWERS   110

CHAPTER 18 FOR FUN ANSWER   114

CHAPTER 19 MORE MATH RIDDLES ANSWER   120

CHAPTER 20 BONUS RIDDLE ANSWERS   125

CONCLUSION   130

Introduction

Riddles turn math into a fun game for your child to latch onto. Puzzling out the solution allows your child to combine math with other important skills like reasoning and persistence.

Getting children to enjoy and fully engage in learning new concepts can be a tricky task. While all kids desire to learn more about the world around them, many of them are alienated by traditional teaching methods that make lessons feel too much like work. Math in particular suffers from lesson plans that go no further than handing out worksheets without any attempt to show children how relevant math really is in their daily lives. In these cases, the best option is to combine work with play. If learning resembles a game, presents a meaningful yet fair challenge, and allows children to flex their critical thinking muscles, children will often find themselves engaged in their education with little trouble.

Math riddles bridge the gap between study and recreation. They combine key principles of giving kids a challenge they can work towards and find intrinsic rewards in completing with the development of arithmetic, pattern recognition, and other mathematical skills. Completing math problems does not have to mean finishing a series of endless equations. Utilizing riddles turns this process into a game that children will naturally want to become better at. In doing so, they will begin to find the value in learning math and similar subjects that may have initially disinterested them. Math riddles can also be a good way for kids more familiar with math concepts to challenge themselves, helping them to receive additional practice and education outside of the classroom. Math riddles have the added benefit of encouraging the whole family to work together to support a child's education no matter their current proficiency.

The math riddles will provide hours of thought provoking and challenging fun for smart kids looking to expand their math knowledge and get ahead in their studies. To understand the power math riddles have and the surprising amount of fun they are to complete, you must first understand what math riddles are and how you can use them to support your child's growth and development.

Whether your kid is a math whiz or they are looking to build their skills, it will allow them to show off their math muscles and establish a strong foundation of mathematical knowledge that will support them through all stages of life.

Chapter 1 Simple Math Riddles

1. If two's company, and three's a crowd, what are four and five?

2. Which is heavier: a ton of bricks or a ton of feathers?

3. The day before yesterday I was 21, and next year I will be 24. When is my birthday?

4. Which weighs more, a pound of feathers or a pound of bricks?

5. How many months have 28 days?

6. What do the numbers 11, 69, and 88 all have in common?

7. Is an older one-hundred-dollar bill worth more than a newer one?

8. If it rains at midnight today, in the next 72 hours, will you see the sunshine?

9. A tailor has a piece of cloth that is 16 feet long and he will cut the fabric by 2 feet per piece every day. In summary, how many days will he spend? Even if the last piece of cloth is cut

10. If there are 5 sewing machines in the factory, can cut 5 T-shirts by using 5 minutes. If there are 100 sewing machines, cut 100 T-shirts. It will take a couple of minutes.

11. There are 3 stalks on the table. How can you change the middle match to another position without touching it?

12. The balloon is being blown away by the wind in the south. Do you know that Flags attached to the basket of balloons In which direction to wave?

13. What question did you ever answer the word "No" once?

14. What symbols should we place between 4 and 5 to make the answer more than 4 but less than 5?

15. A man sitting Even though he stood up You can't compete with him. In conclusion, what is he sitting on?

16. " 1? 17? 3 = 9? 6 " Put a " + " and " - " sign instead of the mark? To get the correct answer By not changing the position of numbers

17. Why is six afraid of seven?

18. There are a certain number of books on my bookshelf. I took a book which is 6th from the right

and 4th from the left. Can you find out the number of books on my shelf?

19. Two fathers, two sons, and a grandfather went to the movies together. Each person bought one movie ticket. How many tickets did they buy in total?

20. A duck had $9; a spider had $36, a bee had $27. Considering this information, how much money would a cat have?

21. If you purchase a rooster to lay eggs and you expect to get two eggs per day for, how many eggs will you have after two weeks?

22. I have a tail and a head, yet I have no legs and body. What am I?

23. The price of eggs is $0.12 a dozen. How many can you purchase for one dollar?

24. A rabbit sees six elephants while he is going to the river. Each elephant sees two monkeys that are going to the river. Each monkey is holding one parrot. How many animals are going to the river?

25. On a faraway planet, half of 10 is 6. With those proportions, what is 1/6th of 30 on this planet?

26. Multiplying this number by any other number, the answer will always be the same. What number is it?

27. If you take Betti's age and multiply it by one and a half times, you get 24. How old is Betti?

28. Saturday, Silvia and Jane went out to lunch. The check was $12 and was divided equally among friends. Silvia paid $4, and Jane paid $4. Who paid the rest?

29. Five friends are in a room and the sum of their ages is 48. Ten years from now, what will the sum of their ages be?

30. A snail is trying to get to the top of a 5-yard pole. During the day the snail goes up 3-yards and at nigh time he goes down 2-yards. How long will it take for him to get to the top of the pole?

31. How many times can you steal a cookie from a jar with 100 cookies inside?

Chapter 2 Easy Math Riddles

These riddles are relatively easy while still keeping your mind hard at work. Starting easy and working your way up to more difficult questions will help you build the confidence and problem-solving skills you will need for later riddles. Flex your math muscles with the following questions.

1. An aquarium has 300 fish. They are looking to remove 45 of their fish and add 80 new ones. How many fish will they have after this?

2. James' dad is three times older than he is. If James is 14, how old is his dad?

3. Greg has a brother named Phil and a sister named Daphne. Phil is seven years old; Daphne is 15 years old, and Greg's age is exactly in between the two of them. What is Greg's age?

4. Harry and his friend Tina go apple picking together at an orchard. Harry picks six apples. Tina picks her apples much faster and ends up with double the number of apples. How many apples did Tina pick?

5. The Birchwood family decides to have a big family gathering. While inviting everyone, they notice that

their family has three times as many girls as it does boys. If there are nine boys, how many girls are there?

6. Jamar invited three of his friends to his house. He wants to split his toys up into equal amounts for each of his friends and himself. If he has 16 toys with him, how many toys should each person get?

7. What number comes next in this pattern? 1, 2, 2, 4, 8, 32, _

8. Janet made $80 mowing lawns over the weekend. She spends half on new shoes on Monday. On Tuesday, she spends $12 on lunch with her friends. Assuming she does not spend any money on Wednesday, how much money does she have left?

9. Coach Ross starts the basketball season with eight basketballs. During the season, one basketball gets a hole in it and deflates. Two basketballs get lost, and one more accidentally goes home with another team. At the end of the season, how many basketballs should Coach Ross buy if he wants to have eight basketballs again?

10. A grocery store stocks 27 cartons of milk. They are running a sale so that they can sell at least a third of what they have in stock. If the sale is successful, how many cartons of milk will be sold?

11. Justin goes to the store to buy a candy bar. The candy bar costs $1.50. If all Justin brought with him is quarters, how many quarters should he give the cashier?

12. Start with the number 10, then subtract three. Now add five. What number is in the ones place of the answer?

13. A chicken lays two eggs each day. At the end of three weeks, how many eggs has the chicken laid?

14. A burger and soda cost $10. If the burger is $2 more than the soda, how much does each item cost?

15. A zookeeper has eight pairs of animals. Each pair has two babies. Of the babies, four are sent to other zoos. How many animals total, including both babies and adults, remain at the zoo?

16. David has $32. He spends half of his money on a new football. After that, he spends half of his remaining money on a new dinosaur toy. How much money does David have left?

17. A number sequence contains the numbers 1, 8, 15, __, 29, and 36. What is the missing number?

18. Josie and her mom go to the grocery store at 2:00 PM. After they get their groceries, they spend another 30 minutes at the laundromat next door, and another 20 minutes at the bank in the same area.

Assume the drive to the grocery store takes 10 minutes and that there was no additional time spent in the car to reach the other stores. If Josie and her mom get home at 4:20 PM, how long did they spend in the grocery store?

19. Leon wants to buy a bag of chips that costs $2.75, but he only has coins with him. If Leon has three quarters, five dimes, and nine nickels, does he have enough money to buy the chips?

20. Kyra plans to run half a mile every day to exercise. If she does this for two weeks, how far will she run altogether?

21. Five friends have breakfast together and all eat different amounts of pancakes. Lisa eats three, Cody eats five, Griffin eats two, Tanya eats four, and Matt eats one. What is the average number of pancakes eaten, and who eats that many?

22. I am thinking of a number between 10 and 20. It is divisible by three, but not by two. What number am I thinking of?

23. John is half the age of his sister. His age is a multiple of two. His sister is younger than 20. If John is older than seven but younger than 11, how old is his sister?

24. The ice cream man starts the day out with 20 ice cream cones. At 10:00 AM, he sells two. At 11:00 AM, he sells three more. At 1:00 PM, he sells double what he sold at 10:00 and 11:00 combined. How many ice creams cones does he have left?

25. What is the next number in the following pattern? 3, 9, 27, 81, _

26. Jason has to complete all of his homework questions before dinner at 6:00 PM. If he starts his homework at 4:00 PM, and he has 30 questions, how long should it take him to answer each question if he wants to stay on track to finish on time?

27. A new baseball bat and glove cost $30. If the bat costs double the cost of the glove, what is the price of each item?

28. A lock is opened by a single number. The note on the back of the lock says that to find the number, you must solve for the difference between 350 and 146 and use the number in the tens place. What number will open the lock?

29. Clarissa's age is one third of her mother's age. If Clarissa's mother is between the ages of 31 and 34, and Clarissa's age is a whole number, what is her age?

30. Larry starts his essay on Monday and wants to finish by the end of the day on Friday. If Larry's essay has to be 500 words, and he writes 120 words each day, will he finish writing his essay on time?

31. I am thinking of a number between 15 and 30. The number does not have a 2 in its ones or tens place. It is a multiple of four. What number am I thinking of?

32. Iris and Dahlia want to see who can get the furthest on the monkey bars. Iris finishes half of the monkey bars, while Dahlia finishes six monkey bars. If there are 10 monkey bars, who got the furthest?

33. Walt has $20. He sets $5 aside on Tuesday and makes sure not to spend it. Then Walt spends $11 on Wednesday. On Thursday, he spends half of what is left. How much money does Walt have left on Friday?

34. Yasmine spends 20 minutes on her math homework, 30 minutes on her reading homework, and 15 minutes on her vocabulary homework. If she started her homework at 3:30 PM, what time does she finish all of her homework?

35. What is the missing number in this pattern? 32, 16, _, 4, 2, 1

36. Calvin is building a model rocket ship. According to the instructions on the box, the rocket ship takes 40 minutes to build. If Calvin starts putting the rocket ship together at 1:30 PM but he has soccer practice at 2:15 PM, will he have time to finish building the rocket ship?

37. Popcorn and soda at the movie's costs $21. If the popcorn costs $5 more than the soda, how much does the popcorn cost? How much does the soda cost?

38. Jacob and Isabelle go shopping together. They begin at the shoe store and spend 25 minutes there. Next, they look at jackets and spend 15 minutes trying them on. Finally, they spend 30 minutes shopping for shirts. If they exit the last store at 4:55 PM, what time did they start shopping? Assume there is no time spent travelling between the stores.

39. Trayvon's sister is four years older than he is plus half of his age. If Trayvon's sister is 10, how old is Trayvon?

40. There are a certain number of chickens in a coop. The number of chickens is smaller than 15, but larger than 10. The number is a multiple of 2. It is not a multiple of 7. How many chickens are in the coop?

41. Gap 30 through $\frac{1}{2}$ and include 10. What's the appropriate response?

42. An assistant on the butcher shop is six toes tall and wears length 10 shoes. What does he gauge?

43. A rancher has 19 sheep on his territory. At some point, a gigantic storm hits and all anyway seven flee. What number of sheep does the rancher have left?

44. Your sock cabinet handiest comprises of 18 white socks and 18 blue socks. How often would you like to reach inside the cabinet and take out a sock to guarantee a coordinating pair?

45. You planted sunflower seeds to your back yard. Consistently, the amount of vegetation copies. On the off chance that it takes fifty-two days for the vegetation to fill the nursery, what number of days would it take for them to fill a large portion of the nursery?

46. Utilizing most straightforward expansion, how might you work eight eights to get the range 1,000?

47. When Ashley got 15, her mom was 37. Presently, her mother is twice her age. How old is Ashley?

Enjoying this book?

Please leave a review because we would love to hear your feedback, opinions and advice to create better products and services for you! Thank you for your support. You are greatly appreciated!" CLICK HERE

Chapter 3 Intermediate Math Riddles

The questions in this section will be a little more difficult than the Ones in the previous section. They will deal with more advanced topics such as factors, fractions, and prime numbers. Minimal amounts of guidance may be necessary to get the answers to these riddles. Consider the last section's questions as a warmup for this section. Now that you understand how to answer the easier math riddles, these 100 riddles will really test your math muscles and allow you to showcase your abilities.

1. Start with the number 100. Divide by two, then add 25. Multiply that number by three. What digit is in the ones place of the answer?

2. When Paul was eight, his sister was 13. Now, he is exactly $\frac{3}{4}$ of his sister's age. It has been less than 10 years since Paul was eight, but it has been more than four years. What age is he now? Assume both of their ages are whole numbers. Sister are between four and 10 years older than they used to be.

3. If there are 60 seconds in a minute, 60 minutes in an hour, and 24 hours in a day, how many seconds are in a day?

4. Take the highest single digit prime number and multiply it by itself. What is the answer?

5. Eggs are $0.50 for a dozen. You must buy eggs by the dozen. How many eggs can you get for $3?

6. One cup of lemonade is ⅙ of a pitcher. If you have four pitchers of lemonade, how many cups can you make? Assume no ice is added to the cups and that all of the cups are the same size.

7. Four friends have a waffle eating contest. Jenny eats three waffles. Terry eats two more waffles than Jenny. Liam eats half the number of waffles that Terry eats. Riley eats three more waffles than Liam eats. Who wins the waffle eating contest?

8. Your sock drawer has six black socks and six white socks. At most, how many times will you have to take a sock out to have a matching pair?

9. Trevor plays baseball and lacrosse. On Tuesdays, he has practice for both sports, one after the other with a break in between. He starts practice at 3:40 PM and ends practice at 5:20 PM. If he spends half of that time at lacrosse practice and a quarter of it at baseball practice, how long is the break in between the two practices?

10. Imagine that instead of the usual amount of time, there are 40 minutes in an hour and 40 seconds in a minute. If this is true, then how many seconds are in three hours?

11. Larissa has $24 from her allowance. She spends a third of her money on a new toy. She spends half of what is left on lunch with her friends. Finally, she spends $2 on some candy. How much money does Larissa have left?

12. A pizza split into eight slices is shared by a group of six friends. They all eat equal amounts of pizza, but first they need to divide the pizza further so everyone can eat the same amount. How should they divide the pizza so everyone can eat equal amounts?

13. The school cafeteria begins the day with 80 cartons of plain milk and 60 cartons of chocolate milk. There are 72 students who buy milk with lunch. A third of them want plain milk, while two thirds want chocolate milk. Is there enough milk for all of the students to get the kind they want?

14. Melanie goes to the store to buy candy by the individual piece. She has only a single dollar. She wants to get as much candy as she can. If a piece of sweet candy costs $0.30, a piece of sour candy costs $0.40, and a piece of chocolate costs $0.50, what kind of candies should Melanie buy to maximize the number of candies she gets? Assume that Melanie has no preference for the

different types of candy and she likes all of them equally.

15. Start with the number 42. Multiply by 0.3, then divide by 0.2. Finally, multiply by four. What is the result of performing these operations?

16. What is the next number in the following pattern? 0, 4, 2, 6, 4, 8, 6, 10, 8, _.

17. Mr. Ace is selling ice cream. He starts the day with 25 ice cream cones. At 12:00 PM, he sells three cones. At 1:00 PM, he sells seven cones. At 2:00 PM, he gets a delivery of 10 more ice cream cones. At 3:00 PM, he sells a fifth of what he has left. He closes at 4:00 PM and makes no more sales for the day. How many ice cream cones does Mr. Ace have left at the end of the day?

18. Polly's dad bakes her a sheet of cookies. However, Polly is only allowed to eat a quarter of the cookies at a time. The rest must be saved for another day. If 12 cookies fit on a sheet, how many cookies can Polly eat?

19. Jonathan's age has the factors two, three, five, six, 10, and 15, as well as one and itself. If Jonathan's age is less than 45, what must his age be?

20. A pair of headphones are $27. Layton wants to save up for the headphones with the allowance he makes each week. He gets $8 as a weekly allowance, but he spends half of it on lunches. If Layton starts with no money

saved up, how many weeks will it take him to be able to afford the new headphones?

21. Dylan has $5.00 to spend on lunch. He buys a sandwich for $2.30, a drink for $1.40, and a snack for $0.75. If a cookie is $1.00, does he have enough lunch money left to get the cookie too?

22. A new camera costs $23.50 more than a roll of film. If film costs $4.50, how much do both items cost together?

23. Miya practices clarinet every day from Tuesday to Friday. On Tuesday, she plays for $\frac{1}{3}$ of an hour. On Wednesday, she practices for $\frac{1}{2}$ of an hour. On Thursday, she is only able to spend $\frac{1}{4}$ of an hour on her clarinet. To make up for it, she plays for $\frac{2}{3}$ of an hour on Friday. How long in minutes has she spent playing clarinet by the end of the day on Friday?

24. Kerrie sells lemonade during the summer. In June, she sells 45 cups. In July, she sells 1.5 times what she sold in June, rounded up to the nearest whole number. If her sales for August are double what she sold in June, how many cups of lemonade does she sell altogether?

25. Julio helped his grandma with chores over the weekend and made $20. He spends a quarter of it on Monday and a third of the remaining money on Tuesday. How much money has he spent?

26. Three friends have a contest to build the highest tower out of cards. Sam's tower has 12 cards. Nancy's tower is equal to the number of cards in Sam's tower plus four, then divided by two. Jaden's tower is equal to the number of cards in Nancy's tower multiplied by three, then minus eight. Who has the winning tower?

27. Leon is in charge of getting snacks for his class. There are 13 students in Leon's class including himself. They must all get an equal number of pretzels. If there are 104 pretzels in a bag, how many pretzels should each student get?

28. Natasha spends five minutes reviewing her vocabulary words. Then she puts the word list away. She gives herself 30 seconds to spell each word from memory before moving to the next one. If she has 20 vocabulary words to learn, how long does she spend on her vocabulary work in minutes?

29. A grocery store sells five watermelons on Thursday and 25 watermelons on Friday. How many times more watermelons did they sell on Friday than on Thursday?

30. Frankie and five of his friends each have $\frac{1}{2}$ of their sandwiches left over from lunch. How many complete sandwiches do they have if they count them all together?

31. Start with 0.5 and add 0.3. Divide by two. Add 0.7. Finally, multiply by 0.5. What number do you get?

32. Diana buys a shirt for $23. While she is checking out, the cashier asks if she would like to donate an additional 20 percent of her purchase to their charity drive. If Diana agrees, what is the new total cost of her purchase?

33. One serving of chips is $\frac{1}{8}$ of a bag. If each serving weighs 1.25 ounces, what is the weight of the entire bag of chips?

34. An aquarium has half as many clownfish as they do blue tangs. They also have a third as many angelfish as they do blue tangs. Without knowing the exact number of any of the types of fish in the aquarium, how do you know if they have more clownfish or angelfish?

35. A cake is already cut into four equal pieces, but three friends want to share the cake. How can they further divide the four slices so that everyone can have an equal amount of cake?

36. What is the missing number in the following sequence of times? 1:30 PM, 1:50 PM, 1:40 PM, 2:00 PM, 1:50 PM, __, 2:00 PM.

37. There are 32 people riding the bus. At the first stop, five people get off the bus and eight people get on. At

the next stop, $\frac{1}{5}$ of the current riders get off and four more get on. How many people are now on the bus?

38. Edward has four bottles of apple juice that are each $\frac{2}{3}$ full. If he pours them all together to take up as few bottles as possible, how many full bottles of apple juice will he have? Will there be any left over?

39. Collin is $\frac{1}{5}$ of his mother's age plus seven. If his mother is 35, how old is Collin?

40. On a 24-hour clock, the numbers run from 00:00 to 23:59, with 00:00 being midnight. 12:00 PM is 12:00, 1:00 PM is 13:00, 2:00 PM is 14:00, and so on. If you are measuring time using a 24-hour clock, what time would 7:30 PM be?

Chapter 4 Moderate Math Riddles

1. Imelda was older than her daughter by 24 years. Two years hence, Imelda will be twice her daughter's age. What is the current age of Imelda's daughter?

2. All of you have seen the telephone number pad. Now, multiply all the numbers together. What will be your answer?

3. If you write twelve thousand, twelve hundred, and twelve in numbers, what will it be?

4. Jessica has gone to buy some clothes in a store that was offering everything at a discount of 25%. If it was a cash payment, there was a further 25% discount offered. What is the amount that Jessica paid entirely in cash for garments worth $100?

5. A class has 22 students and the average age is 21 years. If you included the teacher's age, then the average went up by 1. What is the age of the teacher?

6. How many pieces of cake can you get if you were to cut a cake with just 3 cuts?

7. If you have 24 hours and subtract a day from it, how many seconds are you left with?

8. Three salesmen can sell three cars in seven minutes. At this rate, how many cars can be sold by six salesmen in seventy minutes?

9. A car has one spare tire and four tires which are used on a regular basis. Each tire can travel up to a maximum of 20000 miles before it wears off completely and needs to be changed. What is the maximum distance you can travel in such a car before you have to buy a new tire?

10. Six years ago, the ages of Vincent and Sean were in the ratio of 6:5. Four years from now, the ratio will be 11:10. What is Sean's age now?

11. Presently, the ratio of the ages of Sharon and Sean is 4:3. After 6 years, Sharon will be 26 years old. What is Sean's present age?

12. John is 2/5ths as old as his mother. After eight years, his mother's age will be twice that of his. What is his mother's age today?

13. Find the age of my dad with the following clues: He is thrice my sister's age. My sister is twice my brother's age. My brother is twice my nephew's age. The sum of their ages is an exact multiple of 5 and is less than 100.

14. Sharon's father was 38 years old when she was born. Her mother was 36 years old when her younger sister

(born 4 years after Sharon) was born. What is the age difference between the parents?

15. Suppose you have to choose a door from three doors, out of which hide goats behind them, and one of them has the keys to a luxury car. You have chosen Door No.1. However, before you open it, your host (who knows which door holds what) opens Door No.3, which reveals a goat. So, either Door No. 1 or Door No.2 has the prized keys. Now, if your host allows you to make a switch, is it worthwhile to make the switch or not?

16. Sum-days are those days where the month and the day add up to the year. For example, 01/01/02 is January 01, 2002 which is sum-day because, $1 + 2 = 2$(the year). Using this information, find out what will be the last sum-day in the 21st century?

17. In continuation of Q216, how many sum-days are there in the 21st century?

18. Two girls, Jenny and Penny, participate in a 100m race. Penny wins the race by 5m. To make the race fair, a second race was organized in which Penny was made to start 5m behind Jenny. Who won the second race if both the girls run at the same speed as they ran in the first race?

19. If there are four quadruplets, two twins, and three triplets in your home, how many people are there?

20. Use the following clues to find out how many are yawning and how many are eating. Twice the number of people who are eating = half the number of people who are laughing. 20 people are thinking who are also laughing. $\frac{1}{4}$ of the laughing people are yawning too.

21. There are two trains traveling to New Jersey, one from Boston at 100 mph, and one from Philadelphia at 150 mph. When the trains meet which one will be closer to New Jersey, the one from Boston or the one from Philadelphia?

22. There is a man who needs to ferry across a sack of carrots, a fox, and a rabbit across a river. He can carry only one item at a time. How can you do so without ensuring the rabbit doesn't eat the carrots or the fox doesn't eat the rabbit? The fox and rabbit behave themselves when the man is there to guard them.

23. Three brothers, Adam, John, and David live on a farm. They decided to buy new seeds and split the costs equally amongst themselves. Adam stayed behind to look after the fields while John and David went to buy seeds. John bought 75 sacks of seeds, and Adam bought 45 sacks. The seeds were equally split amongst them, and Adam paid $1400 for his share of the seeds. How much did John and David

each get from this amount so that each paid an equal amount?

24. Complete the following sequence: 1=3, 2=3, 3=5, 4=4, 5=4, 6=3, 7 =?

25. A frog falls into a well that is 14 $\frac{1}{2}$ feet in depth. He starts climbing up. He moves up in the following way: When he jumps up once, he is able to cross 3 feet. But he immediately slips down one foot. In how many jumps will he reach the top? The answer is in jumps, not steps.

26. David said, "Two years hence, my age will be two times what it was five years ago." How old is David?

27. A lady has 7 brothers and each of them has a sister. How many children does the lady have?

28. A street 40 yards long has trees at every 10 feet on both sides. How many trees are there?

29. A 10-feet chain is nailed on the wall in such a way that that the middle of it dips from the place each end of the chain is nailed. How far are the ends of the chain from each other?

30. Do the following subtractions: 9 from 6, 10 from 9, 50 from 40? You will be left with 6. How can this be possible?

31. Devon is two times as old as Kate and half his father's age. Fifty years hence, Kate will be half as old as the father. What is Devon's age now?

32. Complete the following series: 4, 6, 12, 18, 30, 42, 60, 72, 102, 108, ...

33. Find the pair of numbers which satisfies the following equation: xy = yx

34. If the radius of a pizza is 'z' and the depth is 'a', what is the volume of the pizza?

35. One whole fish and one 1/2 fish together weighed 1 $\frac{1}{2}$ pound. The weight of the whole fish and that of the $\frac{1}{2}$ fish was the same. What will be the total weight of the full fish and double the $\frac{1}{2}$ fish (or the whole of the fish which was cut in half)?

36. If you reverse the digits of David's age, you will get his daughter's age. One year ago, David was twice as old as his daughter. What are their present ages?

37. There are 100 applicants for some sales positions in a company. 12 of them have no selling experience at all. 64 of them have experience of selling music equipment. 80 of them have experience selling electronic goods. How many have experience in both?

38. In a farm, the number of sheep is half that of hens. The total number of legs and heads is 187. Find the number of hens and sheep.

39. Find the next in the series: 11, 1331, 161051, 19487171, _____

40. The cost of a banana and an apple is $1.19. The cost of a pear and an apple is $1.45. The cost of a pear and a banana is $1.40. Find the cost of each fruit.

41. Replace 'a' in the following equation with mathematical operators to make it true: 9 a 8 a 7 a 6 a 5 a 4 = 91

42. A man goes to the market with $100 in cash. He has to buy exactly 100 animals, three different kinds of animals and at least one of each. The cost of each animal is as follows: a cow - $15, a chicken – $0.25, and a goose - $1. How does the man make his purchase spending all $100 dollars?

43. Two wine traders bring 64 and 20 barrels of wine each to a trading post. They pay the following duty at the check post: The first man (with 64 barrels) pays a duty of 5 barrels and 40 francs. The second man pays a duty of 2 barrels but gets back 40 francs. What is the cost of each barrel and what was the duty payable?

44. What is the smallest number that has an 'a' in its name?

45. Find the number that will result in 81 if the following operations are done: first add 47, multiply the sum by 3, and divide the resultant product by 2.

46. A shopkeeper has the following sales in 5 consecutive months: $6435, $6927, $6855, $7230, and $6562. What sales must he do in the 6th month so that his average is $6500?

47. A father's and his son's ages total up to 66. The age of the father is determined by reversing the age of the son. There are 3 possible answers. What are they?

48. The average income of Mr. Adam and Mr. Bobby is $5050. The average income of Mr. Bobby and Mr. Crew is $6250. The average income of Mr. Adam and Mr. Crew is $5200. What is the income of Mr. Adam?

Chapter 5 Medium Riddles

1. What is the next number in the pattern? 4, 2, 1, $\frac{1}{2}$, __.

2. An auditorium has 240 seats. Three different classes are brought to the auditorium to watch a guest speaker. Mrs. Price's class has 30 kids, Ms. Jackson's class has 25 kids, and Mr. Maple's class has 25 kids. What fraction of the seats in the auditorium are filled by the three classes altogether?

3. Start with the number 540. Divide by two, then add 25. Subtract 12, then divide by two once more. What number do you get?

4. A chicken lays two eggs every morning and one extra egg on Saturday. Every Sunday, $\frac{2}{3}$ of the eggs the chicken has laid are removed by a farmer. How many eggs remain in the nest after one week has passed?

5. The number of flowers in a garden doubles every day. If the garden starts on day one with four flowers, how many flowers will there be in five days?

6. I am thinking of a number that is greater than 40 but less than 60. It is a multiple of five. The number does not end in a zero. The first digit of the number is not a multiple of four. What number am I thinking of?

7. A farmer has a herd of horses with four different coat colors. $\frac{1}{4}$ of the horses are solid brown, $\frac{1}{4}$ are brown with white speckles, $\frac{1}{4}$ are white with brown speckles, and $\frac{1}{4}$ are solid white. If the farmer chooses a horse at random without looking at its coat color, what are the chances that the horse he chooses will have a coat with at least some brown on it?

8. Three zoos compare the number of flamingos they each have. The first zoo has 64 flamingos. The second zoo has half the number of flamingos the first zoo has. The third zoo has 2.5 times as many flamingos as the second zoo. How many flamingos do zoos two and three have?

9. A city throws a parade and requests that the local florists each provide floats with many flowers. There are four florists in the city. The first float has 368 flowers, the second has 842 flowers, the third has 295 flowers, and the fourth and biggest float has 1243 flowers. How many flowers do all the floats have combined?

10. A cheetah can run 70 miles per hour. If the cheetah runs for 40 minutes, about how far can it get, rounded to the nearest mile, assuming it can maintain the same speed the whole time?

11. Emperor penguins in Antarctica have large migrations every year, but their short legs mean they can only waddle so far each day. If a group of penguins walks four miles every day for three weeks, how far do they get?

12. One pound is equal to 0.0005 tons. How many pounds is one ton to?

13. Ashley helps out at her school's bake sale. Brownies cost $1.50, cookies cost $1.00, and cake pops cost $0.50 each. If she sells eight brownies, 12 cookies, and nine cake pops, how much money does Ashley make for her school?

14. Damian helps his parents cook dinner. They spend 10 minutes washing and cutting up ingredients, 20 minutes assembling the meal, 35 minutes cooking the food, five minutes letting it cool, and finally 40 minutes enjoying the meal. If they finish eating at 6:45 PM, what time did Damian and his parents start working on dinner?

15. A restaurant serves a special that includes five chicken wings, three celery sticks, and a drink. If the restaurant sold 38 of these specials in a night, how many chicken wings, celery sticks, and drinks did they sell?

16. A school cafeteria offers apple juice, orange juice, and water with their lunches. They have 30 bottles of apple juice, 25 bottles of orange juice, and 40 bottles of water. If there are 60 students buying lunch and ⅓ of them want each kind of drink, are there enough drinks of each kind for everyone to get what they want?

17. What is the next number in the following sequence? 100, 200, 150, 300, 250, 500, 450, _.

18. A neighborhood contains 43 families. Nine families move out, then six more move in. Half of the families move out. They are replaced by 26 new families. How many families does the neighborhood now contain?

19. Greg gets 30 pieces of candy on Halloween, but his parents don't want him to eat it all at once. They decide he can have two pieces of candy every day. If he follows the rules, they will give him an extra eight pieces of candy. Assuming Greg follows his parents' rules, how long does it take him to eat all of his candy?

20. Selina's grandmother's age divided by four is 20.5. How old is Selina's grandmother?

21. A cupcake recipe calls for $\frac{3}{4}$ of a cup of sugar to make six cupcakes. If you want to make 24 cupcakes, how many cups of sugar should you use?

22. One big bag of rice weighs six pounds. One cup of rice weighs about $\frac{1}{2}$ pound. If you want to split the big bag of rice into three cup servings, how many different containers will you need?

23. A florist sells three dozen roses for $54. How much does each rose cost?

24. A candle burns at a rate of two inches every twenty minutes. If the candle is 14 inches tall, how long will it take the candle to burn completely?

25. Annalise sent 60 text messages in the last week. She sent 0.2 of her messages on Monday, 0.3 on Tuesday, 0.1 on Wednesday, 0.0 on Thursday, and 0.4 on Friday. How many messages did she send each day?

26. Henry spent 23 hours ice skating this winter. His friend Beth spent 1.5 times as many hours ice skating. How many more hours did Beth spend ice skating than Henry?

27. One basket of fresh oranges weighs 16 pounds. If an unknown number of baskets of oranges weighs 288 pounds, how many baskets of oranges are there?

28. Linda sells her own handmade bracelets for $6.50 apiece. She sells 15 bracelets in her first week. Next week, she sells 1.2 times as many bracelets. How much money did Linda make at the end of the two weeks?

29. Mr. Hopper's daughter is four years younger than ⅓ of his age. If Mr. Hopper is 54, how old is his daughter?

30. Jackie wants to buy gifts for her three friends. She has $44. If she wants to keep the costs of her friends' gifts as equal as possible, what is the highest amount she can spend on any one friend's gift?

Chapter 6 Hard Level Riddles

1. A particular service center receives the maximum number of service calls between three and four in the afternoon. During this period, the number of calls received is 60% more than the 600 calls received between two and three in the afternoon. What is the average number of calls per minute received by the service between three and four in the afternoon?

2. Three coins are tossed up. Two of the three land with their heads facing up. What are the chances of the same thing happening on the next toss?

3. Complete the following number sequence: 1, 5, 13, 29, _____

4. Complete the series: 0, 7, 26, _____

5. Ten years ago, Pat was half of Quentin's age. Today, the ratio between their ages is 3:4. What are their present ages combined?

6. There are many books on a particular shelf. One book's position is 6th from the right and 4th from the left? How many books are there on this shelf?

7. There are 5 children born in 3-year intervals. The sum of their ages is 50. Find the age of the youngest child.

8. You have two special ropes. If you light one end of both the ropes and allow them to burn from end to end, each will take 1 hour. What can you do to ensure that the ropes burn completely in 45 minutes?

9. David told his son, "I was as old as you are now when you were born." If David is 38 years now, how old was his son five years ago?

10. You have 7 balls all of which are absolutely identical except that one of them is slightly lower in weight as compared to the other six. You have a weighing machine and you can weigh only two times. How can you identify the lighter ball?

11. The mileage meter of Mr. John's car read 72927, which is a palindrome; it reads the same forward as well as backward. How many more miles does Mr. John need to travel in order to come to the next palindrome?

12. Complete the sequence: 11, 12, 26 , 81 , 82, 166, 501, 502, 8006, _____

13. John was given a job to do. Each day, he doubles his task. Finally, he completed the job in 18 days. Which

day was it when John completed 25% of the job given to him?

14. Kate is younger than Beck by 7 years. The ratio of their ages is 7:9. How old is Kate?

15. You have 15 cents with you and you go to the local shop to buy toffees each of which costs 1 cent. There is an offer too. You can exchange 3 wrappers for one toffee. What is the maximum number of toffees can you eat with your 15 cents?

16. Kevin's age was four times that of his son, eight years ago. Eight years hence, Kevin will be twice the age of his son. What is Kevin's present age?

17. A man comes to work for you for seven days. Each day you have to pay him 1/7th of a silver bar. He needs to be paid daily. What is the best way to pay him so that there is the least number of cuts needed on the silver bar?

18. Find the number of rungs of the ladder a firefighter is using based on the following clues: He stands at the middle and sprays water on a burning store. He then climbed up 6 rungs to spray water. The heat of the fire made him climb down 10 steps from there. After a few minutes, he was able to climb the remaining 18 rungs to reach the top.

19. A ring with 2 diamonds and 1 stone of ruby was priced at $3000. A set of 4 amethysts and 1 diamond costs $2000. A set with 3 emeralds, 1 amethyst, and 1 diamond costs $1400. If I want a ring with one diamond, one amethyst, one ruby, and one emerald, what will be the cost?

20. 6 b 6 b 66 b 6 b 66 = 113; Put mathematical operators in place of b to make this equation true.

21. You have a thin piece of paper that is 0.0001 m in thickness. If you doubled this paper 50 times, what will be the height of the pile?

22. 2 packets of chocolate chips and 3 packets of jellybeans cost 24 cents. 2 packets of jellybeans and 4 packets of chocolate chips also cost 24 cents. What is the cost of one packet of chocolate chips?

23. Eight daisies and six tulips cost $10. Six daisies and eight tulips cost $11. Calculate the cost of each flower.

24. Find the value of the following: $\frac{1}{2}$ of 2/3 of $\frac{3}{4}$ of 4/5 of 5/6 of 6/7 of 7/8 of 8/9 of 9/10 of 1000

25. Find the length of a fish's head, tail, and middle part with the following measurements: The fish is 15 inches in length. The length of the head is the same as the length of its tail. If the head were two times

as long as it is now, the total length of the tail and head would be equal to that of the middle part.

26. A box of apples can be divided (without cutting or breaking) among 2, 3. or 7 people. What is the minimum number of apples that the box can contain?

27. If you place Rachel's dolls in rows of 3, then one remains. If you lay them in rows of 4, then two remain; in rows of 5, 3 are left, and rows of 6, there are 4 left out. What is the minimum number of dolls that Rachel must have?

28. Julia tells her brother, David, "I have an equal number of brothers and sisters." David responds with, "I have double the number of sisters as I have brothers." How many siblings are there?

29. The weight of a bag of potatoes is 32 pounds divided by half its weight. How much does the bag of potatoes weigh?

30. If I told you that I can add 2 to 11 and get the answer as 1, would you believe me? Think again because this is possible.

31. The average of 20 random numbers is 0. What is the maximum number of these 20 that can be greater than 0?

Math Riddles for Smart Kids

32. A restaurant takes orders for chicken only in 6, 9, and 20 pieces. What is the largest number that you CANNOT order here?

33. A vehicle owner buys fuel at the following rates per liter for three consecutive years: $7.50, $8, and $8.50. He spent $4000 each year towards fuel. What is the average cost of fuel per liter he incurred?

34. In a room of 10 people, if everyone has to shake hands with everyone else, how many total handshakes will take place there?

35. The average number of visitors to a library on Sunday is 510 and on weekdays is 240. What is the average footfall per day in a 30-day month starting with a Sunday?

36. Fill in the missing number: 12, 25, 49, 99, 197, 395, _____

37. A student was marked 83 instead of 63 on one of his exam papers which reduced the average marks of the class by half. Calculate the number of students in the class.

38. There is a 100-kilo melon lying out in the sun. The water content in the melon is 99%. After being out for a long time, the water content reduced to 98%. How much water has evaporated from the melon?

39. Complete the series: 2, 7, 10, 22, 18, 37, 26, _____

40. The average weight of Adam, Bennet, and Cole is 45 pounds. The average weight of Bennet and Cole is 43 pounds and that of Adam and Bennet is 40 pounds. What is the weight of Bennet?

41. A boat moving at 15 mph in still water goes downstream 30 miles and returns in $4 \frac{1}{2}$ hours. What is the velocity of the stream?

42. You have to measure 15 minutes with an 11-minute hourglass and a 13-minute hourglass. How will you do it?

43. Complete the series: 2, 3, 6, 0, 10, -3, 14, _____

44. The difference in the ages of two girls is 16 years. Six years ago, the elder girl was thrice as old as the younger girl. What is the current age of the elder girl?

45. A 130m long train traveling at a speed of 45 mph crosses a bridge in 30 seconds. What is the length of the bridge?

46. I have some loose coins in my pocket, and I cannot change for a nickel, dime, quarter, a half dollar, or a dollar. What is the largest sum of money I can hold that fits this condition?

47. A rich man was distributing money to the needy. He said, 'If there were five people fewer than now, then each of you would have gotten $2 more.' As soon as

he said this, four more people joined the needy group. Now, each of them received $1 less. How much did each person receive?

48. Point out the odd number from this series: 1, 8, 27, 64, 125, 196, 216, 343

49. A, B, and C are natural numbers such as 3A+5B+7C is a perfect square; what are the numbers?

50. You have to carry 3000 apples from the apple farm to the market, which is 1000 miles away. Your vehicle can carry only 1000 apples at a time. You have to pay one apple per mile as duty when you are traveling towards the market. There is no duty for the reverse journey. How many apples at the most can you get to the market?

Chapter 7 Challenging Math Riddles

The riddles will be more challenging. There are 100 riddles that will test your mathematical and logical reasoning skills while still being fair and clear enough to ensure you can arrive at the right answer with a bit of effort. Parental or teacher assistance may be needed for some of the riddles in this, though none are meant to completely stump you. This encourages family involvement in child development as parents can help guide their kids through the problem. The riddles will put your skills to the test and show off just how much of a math master you really are.

1. A zoo is planning a new tiger exhibit. The exhibit's area needs to be 143 square feet. If the exhibit is shaped like a rectangle and the length is two feet longer than the width, how long should each side of the exhibit be?

2. Eggs are $0.24 for a dozen. You must buy eggs by the dozen. How many eggs can you get with $1?

3. A square playground has one side that measures 11 feet. What is the perimeter of the playground?

4. Mikayla's mom orders cold cuts at the deli counter. She gets $\frac{1}{2}$ pound turkey, $\frac{1}{4}$ pound ham, $\frac{1}{4}$ pound salami, and $\frac{3}{4}$ pound cheddar cheese. How many total pounds of cold cuts did Mikayla's mom get from the deli counter?

5. There is a survey to find out how many deer are in big national parks. Six different parks report that they have 1,283, 2,462, 947, 1,672, 2,843, and 1,856 deer respectively. How many deer live in the six parks total?

6. A scientist has hamsters he labels A, B, and C. He wants to know the weight of each hamster, but he can only weigh them in pairs. Hamsters A and B weigh seven pounds, hamsters A and C weigh nine pounds, and hamsters B and C weigh 10 pounds. If he knows hamster A weighs three pounds, how heavy are the other two hamsters?

7. A shelter has 72 cats. $\frac{1}{4}$ are orange, $\frac{1}{4}$ are white, $\frac{1}{8}$ are white with orange patches, $\frac{1}{8}$ are black, and $\frac{1}{4}$ are brown with stripes. How many cats at the shelter do not have a solid fur color?

8. An aquarium wants to put in a new rectangular fish tank that is 14 feet long by 16 feet wide. The glass they use for the tank costs $8 per foot. If the aquarium has a budget of $400, do they have enough money for the size fish tank they want?

9. What is the missing number in the following pattern?
545, 109, _, 4, 36, 0.872

10. A rectangular picture frame is 3.5 inches wide by 4.6 inches long. What is the area of the picture frame in square inches?

11. Start with the number 854. Divide by four. Multiply by $\frac{1}{2}$. Add 53.4. Multiply by 3.2, then subtract 41. What number do you end up with?

12. A bottle of apple white grape juice contains apple juice and white grape juice in different amounts. If the bottle is 3/12 apple juice, how much white grape juice does it contain in its most simplified fraction form?

13. The area of a triangular fence is 32.5 square feet. If the base of the triangle is five feet, what is the height?

14. The heights of two trees in a forest are measured. Their combined height is 64.25 feet. If one tree is four feet taller than the other, how tall are each of the trees?

15. What is the next number in this sequence? 2, 4, 8, 32, 256, _.

16. How can you use addition, subtraction, multiplication, and/or division to get three, seven, and nine to equal 20?

17. Terry's mom makes cookies, but she gives Terry rules for how many he can eat. The number of cookies Terry eats must be between zero and ten. It must be a prime number. The number of cookies he eats multiplied by two should be less than 14. Terry wants to have as many cookies as possible while still following the rules. How many cookies can Terry eat?

18. Kennedy is practicing his running so he can run the mile. On Tuesday, he runs 3.5 laps in four minutes and 30

seconds. On Wednesday, he runs 3,960 feet in three minutes and 45 seconds. If each lap is 1,320 feet, on which day did Kennedy run the fastest?

19. A sheep pen has to be big enough for the sheep to roam and graze freely. If a rectangular pen has a width of 52 feet and a length that is equal to 1.5 times the width, what is the area of the pen?

20. Owen wants to buy a new pack of baseball trading cards. The cards cost $8.75 with a sales tax of seven percent. If Owen has $10, does he have enough money to buy the cards?

21. After a party, $\frac{1}{4}$ of James' birthday cake is left over. If James eats $\frac{1}{3}$ of what remains, what fraction of the total birthday cake did he eat?

22. A lawn care company can mow four lawns in an hour. If a neighborhood has 81 houses and $\frac{2}{3}$ of them want their lawns mowed, how long will it take the lawn care company to finish all of their work?

23. Trisha buys a new computer for $980. She gets a payment plan that allows her to pay the computer off by making monthly payments. If she finishes paying off the computer in a year, how much did she pay each month?

24. A forest contains 685 snakes. 20 percent are black, 40 percent are brown, 15 percent are red and black striped,

and 25 percent are red. How many snakes in the forest are at least partially black?

25. There are 32 containers, each ⅔ full of water. If you poured all of the water together to use the fewest number of containers, how many containers of water would you have?

26. A spinner is made up of thirteen sections of different colors. Four sections are blue, three are red, two are green, and four are yellow. You win if the spinner lands on red or yellow, but it's only a good idea to play if there is a 50 percent or better chance you will win. Should you play?

27. Mount Everest is the tallest mountain peak in the world, at 29,029 feet. The second tallest mountain peak is K2, which stands at 28,251 feet tall. How many feet taller is Mount Everest than K2?

28. Three friends eat different amounts of their own personal pizzas. Gina eats ⅔ of her pizza, Ronald eats ½, and Kyle eats ⅗. Who eats the most pizza?

29. A rectangular house has an area of 825 square feet. If one side of the house is 33 feet, what are the dimensions of the house?

30. A batch of 16 cookies calls for 0.75 cups of sugar. If you want to make 100 cookies, how much sugar do you need rounded to one decimal place?

31. Cookies need to cook for about 11 minutes per batch. You bake two batches, take a 35-minute break, then bake the other 4.25 batches. If you put the first batch in the oven at 11:30 AM, what time is the final batch done?

32. A box can hold up to 23 pounds. Steve packs a lamp that weighs four pounds and eight ounces, a large candle that weighs six pounds and four ounces, and a pumpkin that weighs ten pounds and thirteen ounces. If there are 16 ounces in a pound, how much more weight can the box hold?

33. How can you use addition, subtraction, multiplication, and/or division to make three, four, five, and six equal 70?

34. When weighed together, two boxes weigh six pounds. If one box weighs 16 ounces more than the other, how much do the boxes weigh in ounces? One-pound equals 16 ounces.

35. Emma's mother is making a big pot of chicken soup. She uses six cups of chicken stock. If the recipe makes 24 bowls of soup, how much chicken stock goes into each bowl?

36. A grocery store gives out free samples of apple juice. The sample cups hold four ounces of juice, while a whole bottle holds four cups. If the store hands out 246 free samples, how many bottles of juice did they use? There are eight ounces in a cup.

37. A triangular fence has sides of all different lengths. The first side is equal to the largest single digit prime number. The second side is equal to 1.5 times the first side. The third side is the average of the other two sides. What is the perimeter of the fence in feet?

38. A cupcake weighs 2/13 of a pound. If you put four cupcakes in a box that weighs 1/13 of a pound, how much does the box of cupcakes weigh?

39. A zoo has a koala exhibit and a kangaroo exhibit. They have 34 kangaroos. The number of koalas is double the number of kangaroos. The kangaroo exhibit has an area of 82 square feet. For every extra animal in an exhibit, four square feet must be added. What is the area of the koala exhibit?

40. Paula weighs three different fruits together at the grocery store. An apple and banana weigh 9.75 ounces, while a banana and orange weigh 9.25 ounces. If an apple weighs 5.25 ounces, how much does each fruit weigh?

Chapter 8 For Fun

1. In a bag, there are 60 balls of different colors including blue, red, and green. The number of red balls is four times that of green balls. The number of blue balls is more than the number of green balls by 6. Find out the number of balls of each color.

2. A duck received $8, a bee received $24, and a spider got $32. Using the same logic, how much money will a lion get?

3. Gerry bought some oranges on Tuesday and ate 1/3 of them the same day. The next day, he ate half of what was remaining. On the third day, he looked into the bag and found only 2 oranges left. How many oranges did he buy on Tuesday?

4. Find the number using the following clues: if you add 47 to the number, then multiply the sum by 3, and then divide the product by 2, the answer will be 81.

5. Sandra is 54 years and her mother, Sarah, is 80 years today. How many years ago was Sarah's age thrice that of Sandra's?

6. Frances is 8 years older than her brother. Three years hence, she will be twice her brother's age. What are their ages now?

7. There is a technique which you can use to check if a glass is perfectly half-full or not. It looks more or less half-full. But how can you find if it is exactly half-full? Do you know the technique?

8. You have been given two numbers; 2 and 11. Now you must add something to it so that you can get 1. What is the answer?

9. Peter's father is four times as old as his son. After 8 years, the father will be $2\frac{1}{2}$ times as old as Peter. What will be his age after a further 8 years?

10. A huge ship is anchored off the coast. There is a ladder hanging over the ship with its last rung just touching the water. There is a gap of 20 cm between each rung and the ladder itself is 2 m in length. Now, when the tide rises, the water level goes up at the rate of 10 cm per hour. When will the 5th rung of the ladder be underwater?

11. The current ages of Sam and Peter are in the ratio 5:4. Three years from now, the ratio will be 11:9. What are their present ages?

12. What is the angle that is formed between the hour hand and the minute hand when the time is 3:15?

13. Adam's age is 1/6th that of his father. After 10 years, Adam's father's age will be twice that of Sharon. If Sharon celebrated her eighth birthday two years ago, then what is Adam's present age?

14. You have to go to your granny's house for which you will need to cross 5 bridges. You are planning to take cakes for your granny. Now, at each bridge, the family that manages the bridge requires you to give half of whatever you are carrying to them. In return, they give you back one item from what you have given. How many cakes will you have to carry so that you have two left for your granny after crossing the five bridges?

15. Bobby climbs up a 2-mile hill at 2 mph, and he climbs down the hill at 6 mph. What is Bobby's average speed of climbing up and down the hill?

16. You have to pay an employee working for you for 5 days with pieces of gold that are to be cut from a gold bar. You need to pay him every day for his work. How can you ensure that you complete his payment of gold so that each day, you pay him 1/5th and by ensuring you make the fewest number of cuts?

17. A father-son duo's current ages total up to 60 years. The father was five times as old as his son, six years ago. What will be the son's age six years from now?

18. A newspaper has 16 sheets that are folded in half and has 64 pages in total. The first sheet has pages 1, 2, 63, and 64. If you pick up a sheet with a page number 45, what are the other page numbers you will find in this sheet?

19. David was canoeing on a river at a constant speed. After 6 miles, the wind blew his hat away, and it fell into the stream. As he thought there was no way he would be able to recover his hat, David continued to paddle upstream for another 6 miles before turning back. He rowed at the same speed while returning too. On his return trip, he overtook his hat at the same spot where he started his journey eight hours before. What is the velocity of the river?

20. The current ages of three people are in the ratio 4:7:9. Eight years ago, their ages added up to 56. Find out their current ages.

21. There are 7 people who need to occupy a row of 7 chairs. In how many different ways can this be done?

22. A's age is exactly between that of B and C. The total of B and C ages is 50. Is it possible to find the age difference between A and B?

23. You have been given 5 bottles of pills. One of the bottles contains all contaminated pills which should be discarded. The weight of each good pill is 10 gm

and the weight of each contaminated pill is 9 gm. You have been given a weighing scale to find out the contaminated pill bottle. How will you do it?

24. A length of cloth is colored as follows: 1/3 and $\frac{1}{4}$ of the cloth is colored black and the remaining 8 m is colored gray. Can you find the length of the cloth?

25. Find the 4th equation based on the logic of the first three equations: 8 + 2 = 16106. 5 + 4 = 2091. 9 + 6 = 54153. 7 + 3 =?

26. I was returning from my old aunt's house in her very old car that gave a mileage of 20 miles per gallon. I kept a steady speed of 30 mph. At the beginning of the journey, there were exactly 10 gallons of fuel in the tank. The petrol tank was leaky, too, and the car lost $\frac{1}{2}$ a gallon of fuel every hour. I just made it to my house when the car stopped, as the fuel was totally exhausted. What is the distance of my house from my aunt's house?

27. Diophantus is believed to have used algebraic expressions for the first time. Here is some interesting information about him: His youth lasted 1/6th of his entire life. He decided to grow his beard after 1/12th more. He married after 1/7th more. 5 years after his marriage, he had a son. The son lived half as long as Diophantus did. Diophantus died 4

years after his son died. Use the above information to calculate how long Diophantus lived.

28. The cook prepared 55 same-sized bowls with equal quantities of food in each one of them with the following information regarding the people who were going to eat: Every person gets his or her bowl of soup. Every two persons should share a bowl of spaghetti. Every three persons should share a bowl of salad. All the people eating should eat their own portions of soup, salad, and spaghetti. How many people ate the 55 bowls of food?

29. Find the number of steps this monk climbs every day based on the following daily ritual he follows: He climbs exactly halfway and meditates for one minute. He climbs up a further 8 steps after this, turns east, and waits until he hears a bird sing. He climbs down 12 steps, picks up a pebble. He climbs up one step and throws this pebble over the left shoulder. Now, he takes the remaining steps 3 at a time and for this, he needs only 9 paces

30. Ten years ago, a father was three times as old as his son. Ten years from now, he will be twice that of his son's age. What is the ratio of their current ages?

31. In a class of boys and girls, the number of girls who wear a watch is twice the number of girls who don't wear a watch. The number of boys who don't wear a

watch is double the number of boys who wear a watch. The number of girls in the class is twice the number of boys? How many students are there in the class if the number is between 20 and 32?

32. You have a small piece of paper that measures 10 * 10 cm (area is 10 cm2). Without cutting the paper, how can you halve the area of the same piece of paper?

33. I purchased four items from a store and the cost of three of the items was $1.50, $3.00, and $4.00. Find the price of the fourth item based on the following clue: whether you add the four prices or multiply them together, you will get the same answer.

34. Using only 2s, find an arithmetical expression that will give an answer of exactly 5. Of course, you can use any mathematical operators you want.

35. In a digital clock, what is the smallest interval between two times that appear as palindrome numbers?

36. Arrange the digits 1 to 9 on a tic-tac-toe board in such a way that the rows, columns, and the diagonals total 15.

37. A certain number of children are standing in an evenly spaced circle in such a way that the 7th kid is

standing directly opposite the 18th kid. How many are in the circle?

38. Gerry started peeling 44 potatoes. He peeled at the rate of 3 per minute. After four minutes, Carl joined him and peeled at the rate of 5 per minute. At the end of the job, how many did each of them peel?

39. A man forgot the code to his building. However, he remembered the following clues: The sum of the 5th and 3rd numbers added up to 14. The 4th number is one more than the 2nd number. The 1st number is one less than two times the 2nd number. The sum of the 2nd and 3rd numbers adds up to 10. The sum of all five digits of the code is 30. Can you find out his 5-digit code?

40. Teddy needed to make $52 by selling smoothies at $2 per glass or at $4 for three glasses. He set up shop outside his house and had his $52 by selling 32 glasses of smoothies. How many smoothies did he sell at $2?

Chapter 9 More Math Riddles

1. A businessman bought a horse for 10 baht and sold it for 20 baht and then bought the same horse for 30 baht and sold it for 40 baht. Question: Businessmen will profit from selling horses 2 times. How much is the money?

2. One hotel has 7 floors with 4 people on the ground floor. And each of the next floors will always have more people than the previous two. Question: Which floor will be the most lifted?

3. You have 2 ropes with 1 lighter. If you light a fire at the end of a rope and wait for it to burn out, it will take 1 hour. Question: How do you burn all the ropes in 45 minutes?

4. There is a challenge for everyone to jump over a pencil placed on the floor. But no one can do it. Question: Why?

5. You will use any method that can throw a tennis ball and let it float back to you. Without others helping. Nike experienced a big problem after setting up factories in Africa. Because many shoes were stolen from the factory but then Nike was able to solve this

problem without having to add security measures. Question: How can Nike do it?

6. When did you look at number 2 and say 10. A farmer buys four buffalo. Three buffalo can conceive a normal farmer. There is only one body that cannot conceive despite being strong and unproductive. Question: Why can't this buffalo become pregnant?

7. One brother said "Two years ago, I was 3 times the age of my brother and 3 years. I would be 2 times older than my brother." Question: How old are they now?

8. At a psychiatric hospital there is one doctor and many patients. After the patient has taken the new drug there will be strange side effects that the patient will try to bite another person once a day. Fortunately, this side effect is effective for just one week. Each patient has a wound that is bitten by 2 different lesions, but the doctor is bitten 100 times. Question: How many patients in this hospital?

9. One patient in a psychiatric hospital He often lied about himself. Each day he often lied that he had a different career. The doctor said that if he solved the problem at the doctor Show that he really has that career and the doctor will release him home. The patient said that He is a blacksmith. The doctor therefore gives 5 chains. Each line has 3 rings.

Doctor, let him bring it together in one line. Which patients can do successfully He also split the loop out only 3 rings, so he went home immediately? Question: What can this patient do?

10. George Smith, a wealthy man who was murdered on Sunday evening. Within Mr. Smith's home at that time, there were 5 other people living, including Mrs. Smith, his wife, his personal chef, butler, housekeeper and gardener when Detective Stevens arrived. He asked everyone what he was doing at the scene. And each person's answer is as follows. Mrs. Smith is reading a book near the fireplace. The chef is doing breakfast. Butler is introducing workers in the living room. Housewives are washing dishes in the kitchen. The gardener is watering plants in the glass house. After everyone told what they were doing Detective Stevens was able to immediately capture suspiciousness. Question: Who is lying? And why Detective Stevens knows?

11. Mr. and Mrs. Clyde Flew to travel in France to climb a mountain, but 2 days later, Clyde came home alone with grief He informed the police that his wife had fallen to the top of his death. The next day, Detective Stevens goes to find Clyde to arrest him. Because he was suspected of murdering his wife He confessed his confession. And asked the detective how he knew he was a murderer. Detective Stevens

said He just called to ask the travel company that made the trip to Mr. Clyde and asked some information. Question: Detective Stevens knows exactly what the travel company is?

12. There was a man traveling with 2 sheep and 1 wolf. The wolf would eat the sheep if he left it alone with the sheep. When traveling at one point of the river There is a boat parked, He decided to take all the animals across the land. But the ship can only carry one animal at a time. Question: How can he take all the animals across? Without letting the wolf eat the sheep?

13. A man stabbed his wife until his life. But no one found her body He left her body on the floor and threw a knife that was bloody into the forest. Then drove to work until 1 hour later. The police called him. Along with saying "Your wife has died disturbing you to the scene of the accident "after the husband traveled to the scene the police immediately arrested him. Question: Why does the police know that the husband is a criminal?

14. One sailor there is a cloth attached to a single piece, a length of just 16 feet. Every day, he will cut the fabric off 2 feet per day. Question: How many days does he have to spend? How to cut the fabric completely? Jane doesn't like his own son-in-law. But

every day she will cook for him to eat every day one day She made grilled meat to sit and eat with her son-in-law. She cut in half for the son-in-law. The other half she ate herself After a while, the son-in-law had a pale face. And became blue before the breath. Question: How can Jane survive the poison she put into the meat?

15. There are only 3 doors for you to choose to open. The first one had a killer waiting. The second one has a lion that has not eaten for 3 years and is waiting for you. The third panel is the eternal fire that will drown on you as soon as it is opened. Question: Which one is the safest?

16. There are 4 prisoners attend art classes that the prison provides every Monday. By having the guards escort to the class individually and will be searched every time after class. & Nbsp; They keep their art supplies in the cell. Question: Who are the 4 most likely people to escape from prison?

17. Detective Stevens is talking to a doctor in the waiting room. Suddenly suddenly There was a man running to him and shouting, "Detective, someone shot my wife!" Detective Stevens began to inquire about the man who claimed Clark's name and he told him everything. Clark says "I was at work when the housewife telephoned to tell me that there was an

incident with my wife. And now she is in the emergency room After that, I immediately put up the line and rushed to the hospital immediately. " After Mr Clark finished speaking the detective immediately caught him because he was a suspect trying to kill his wife. Question: Why count Stevens to do that?

18. Larry starts his essay on Monday and wants to finish by the end of the day on Friday. If Larry's essay has to be 500 words, and he writes 120 words each day, will he finish writing his essay on time?

19. I am thinking of a number between 15 and 30. The number does not have a 2 in its ones or tens place. It is a multiple of four. What number am I thinking of?

20. Iris and Dahlia want to see who can get the furthest on the monkey bars. Iris finishes half of the monkey bars, while Dahlia finishes six monkey bars. If there are 10 monkey bars, who got the furthest?

21. Walt has $20. He sets $5 aside on Tuesday and makes sure not to spend it. Then Walt spends $11 on Wednesday. On Thursday, he spends half of what is left. How much money does Walt have left on Friday?

22. Yasmine spends 20 minutes on her math homework, 30 minutes on her reading homework, and 15 minutes on her vocabulary homework. If she started her

homework at 3:30 PM, what time does she finish all of her homework?

23. What is the missing number in this pattern? 32, 16, _, 4, 2, 1

24. Calvin is building a model rocket ship. According to the instructions on the box, the rocket ship takes 40 minutes to build. If Calvin starts putting the rocket ship together at 1:30 PM but he has soccer practice at 2:15 PM, will he have time to finish building the rocket ship?

25. Popcorn and soda at the movie's costs $21. If the popcorn costs $5 more than the soda, how much does the popcorn cost? How much does the soda cost?

26. Jacob and Isabelle go shopping together. They begin at the shoe store and spend 25 minutes there. Next, they look at jackets and spend 15 minutes trying them on. Finally, they spend 30 minutes shopping for shirts. If they exit the last store at 4:55 PM, what time did they start shopping? Assume there is no time spent travelling between the stores.

27. Trayvon's sister is four years older than he is plus half of his age. If Trayvon's sister is 10, how old is Trayvon?

28. There are a certain number of chickens in a coop. The number of chickens is smaller than 15, but larger

than 10. The number is a multiple of 2. It is not a multiple of 7. How many chickens are in the coop?

29. Jackie wants to finish her book by the weekend. The book is 125 pages. If she starts reading on Monday and reads the same number of pages every day, planning on finishing the book on Friday, how many pages should she read each day?

30. Start with the number 25. Add six, then subtract nine. Divide the number by two. What number do you end up with?

31. There are a certain number of rain jackets hanging up on hooks in a row. If one of the rain jackets is third from the left and also seventh from the right, how many rain jackets are hanging up?

32. An aquarium has five male and female pairs of sharks. If each of the pairs have three babies, how many sharks will the aquarium have altogether?

33. What is the next number in the following pattern? 6, 12, 18, 24, 30, _

34. Jared finishes running a mile in eight minutes. Sarah runs the same mile, but she times herself in seconds. She finishes the mile in 540 seconds. Who ran the faster mile?

35. Christina loves playing basketball. In basketball, a normal basket is worth two points, a free throw is

worth one point, and a basket thrown from past the three-point line is worth three points. During her basketball game, Christina makes three normal baskets, two free throws, and one basket past the three-point line. How many points does Christina score?

36. Mrs. Driscoll is trying to decide what homework she should assign her class. She has three different math worksheets. The worksheet one takes 10 minutes to complete. Worksheet two takes 14 minutes. Worksheet three takes 16 minutes. Mrs. Driscoll wants her students to spend less than 30 minutes on their homework, but she wants them to complete at least two worksheets. What combinations of worksheets could she assign to her students?

37. I am thinking of a two digit number. The first digit is smaller than two. The second digit is larger than eight. What is the only number my number could be?

38. If you start with four and subtract or divide by this number, you get the same result. In fact, you get the number itself as the answer. What number is this true for?

Enjoying this book?

Please leave a review because we would love to hear your feedback, opinions and advice to create better products and services for you! Thank you for your support. You are greatly appreciated!" CLICK HERE

Chapter 10 Bonus Riddle

1. A boy was eight years old on his first birthday. Is this possible?

2. Nancy took 9 tests each with a maximum score of 100. Her average is 68. If she removed her lowest score, what will be the highest possible average?

3. A drawer has 10 black and 10 red socks. How many should you pick up without seeing the color to make sure you get one matching pair?

4. William and Sharon buy one small (5 slices) veggie pizza and one medium (8 slices) pepperoni pizza. Sharon, who is a vegetarian, ate four times the number of slices that William ate. How many slices did she eat?

5. How can you make 2, 2, and 2 become 3?

6. Identify this polygon: it has 4 equal sides, the total of its angles is 360, and it is not a square.

7. If you were to write down eleven thousand eleven hundred and eleven in numbers, how will it look?

8. Find out the only three numbers, which will behave as follows: add the first two and the result will be the third.

9. Find the 4-digit number based on the following clues: The third digit is one more than the first digit. The first digit is twice the last digit. The last digit is 10 less than 8 plus the first digit. The second digit is the sum of the other three digits minus 2

10. What 3 consecutive numbers add up to 9000?

11. A fish's tail is as long as a quarter of its body plus its head. Its body is 3/4th of its length. The head of the fish is 4 inches long. What is the length of the fish?

12. Robert has five shirts in blue, red, green, black, and yellow. He has 3 pairs of trousers and 4 hats in blue, red, black, and green. How many full sets of clothes can he make?

13. Note the following equations: 55 = 131, 90 = 194, -35 = -31, 10 = 50, -50 = -58. Using the same logic, with which number will the two sides be equal?

14. Which is that geometrical object that looks the same whether it is spinning around or simply standing?

15. The sequence 425260376469080434957 is unique. Can you identify the uniqueness?

16. A square of side 4 cm is inscribed inside a circle. Can you find the radius of the circle?

17. There are three friends, Andrea, Bobby, and Cat, whose ages have the following relations: Andrea is two years older than Bobby. Bobby is twice as old as Cat. The total of their ages is 27. Find Bobby's age.

18. There are many sandwiches on the table made by Ms. Bennet for her friends. As she counted, she realized that she can share all the sandwiches with 2 friends equally and have nothing for herself. Similarly, 3, 4, 5, and 6 friends could each have an equal number of sandwiches, and there will be none left for Ms. Bennet. What is the minimum number she would have made?

19. Robert is 40 years old and Bobby is 13. How many years ago was Robert four times as old as Bobby?

20. Three people are running a multiple-lap race. Benny finishes one lap in 3 minutes. Trent finishes a lap in 6 minutes, and John completes it in 9 minutes. After what time will the three be at the same starting point?

21. In a game, I lost 50% of my money first, and then gained back 50% of my money. I am still short by $50. What was the amount I started the game with?

22. Rupert has 3 jugs each of which have the following capacity: The first one can hold 9 cups of water. The second one 6 cups. The third one 4 cups. How can he use these three jugs to measure out exactly 7 cups of water?

23. Find a 3-digit number which when reversed results in a larger number and the product of the two numbers is 224455?

24. Michael rents a car to and from the airport. Exactly halfway to the airport, he picks up a friend who returns in the car in the evening. The total rent is $20. The friends decide to split the cost in a fair manner. How much will each pay?

25. There is a number which when multiplied by 9 or any of its multiples will result in answers that have only the multiplication factor. What is this number?

26. Terry ate 50 oranges, David ate half of what Terry ate, Sean ate 1/5th of what David ate, and Hugh ate twenty times as much as Sean. How many oranges did Hugh eat?

27. On the first homework assignment, Kylie got only one star. She wants to get an average of 4 stars. How many more assignments does she need to get 5 stars in order to achieve the 4-star average?

28. An old card game, which is a huge favorite in my family, was invented one year after my dad was born and one year before my mom was born. My oldest parent's age is between 20 + 19 and 82/2. How long ago was this card game invented?

29. In a university, there are 126 freshmen, 375 sophomores, 293 third-year students, and 187 students are in the 4th year. If any one student at the university was to be randomly given an award, what are the chances that it will be a 4th-year student?

30. There are 50 members in a club of superstitious people and 14 more were inducted recently. The leader proposed a toast to the inductees. Every member has 500 ml of wine in his or her glass. How much wine was consumed at the toast?

31. At present, Susan's age is 4/5th of her sister Katherine. Three years ago, Susan's age was half of Katherine. Five years from now, Susan will be 9/10th of her sister. How old are they now if both of them are below 10?

32. A pole is stuck in a lake in such a way that half of it is inside the ground, 1/3rd of it is covered in water, and the rest of 9 ft is outside the water. What is the length of the pole?

33. It was somewhere between 2 pm and 3 pm. Harold's mother asked him to look at the clock and tell her the time as she was in the kitchen and she couldn't see the clock. He said a time that was actually 55 minutes earlier than the real time. His mother realized that something was not right and came out to see and noticed that Harold had mistaken the hour hand to be the minute hand and vice versa. What was the correct time?

34. Calculate the number of days in a 400-year period.

35. Robert has a new fan to fight off the extreme summer heat. The maximum speed at which this fan can run is 40 mph. It is controlled by a knob that can be turned around 360 degrees. Suppose the fan is running at 15 mph, how many degrees would you have to turn the knob to get a constant speed of 25 mph?

36. There is a number which when multiplied by or added to 1.5 gives the same result. What number is this?

37. Janet was 10 years old when Andrew was born. Janet's cousin was 17 years old when she had Andrew. Now, Andrew's mother is 47. How old are Janet and Andrew?

38. Find the number that is less than 3000 and behaves as follows: When divided by 2, leaves a remainder of 1. When divided by 3, leaves a remainder of 2. When

divided by 4, leaves a remainder of 3. When divided by 9, leaves a remainder of 9

39. A 10-ft plank had to be cut into 10 equal sections. Each section took one minute to be cut. How long will it take to get all the 10 sections cut and ready?

40. What is half of 2 plus two equals to?

41. A lady walks into a grocery store and pays $100 to buy an item for $20. The shopkeeper has no change, so he walks into the neighboring shop and gets some change. He then returns $80 and gives her the $20 item as well and the lady leaves. After an hour, the neighbor shop owner comes in and tells the grocery shop owner that the $100 he gave was a counterfeit. The latter exchanges it for a good note. Now, the question is how much money has the grocery shop owner lost?

42. A trader can send 10 small boxes or 8 big boxes in one shipping carton. In one particular shipment, he sent 96 boxes in total with more big boxes than small boxes. How many cartons did he use?

43. There is a super-athlete who can jump forever without stopping. But there is a hitch. After every jump, she gets tired, and her next jump is only half of her previous. Her first jump is $\frac{1}{2}$ of a foot; her second jump, therefore, is $\frac{1}{4}$ of a foot; her third jump

is 1/8 of a foot, and so forth. When will she complete her one-foot jump?

44. There is a 3-digit number, which will give you the same result whether you divide it by 5 or subtract 5 from it. Guess the number? Hint: it is a decimal number

45. The teachers from the math department of a school were having a farewell party for a retiring colleague with the cost being shared equally. Each teacher paid $30. One puzzle-lover among the teachers said, "We are lucky that we are not fewer by five. Else, each of us would have had to pay $10 more." How many teachers were splitting the cost, and what was the cost of the party?

46. If 6 mathematicians took 12 minutes to solve 12 math problems, how long will it take one of them to solve 60 problems?

Chapter 11 Simple Math Riddles Answers

1. Nine

2. Neither—they both weigh a ton.

3. December 31; today is January 1.

4. Neither. They both weigh one pound.

5. All 12 months.

6. The read the same right side up and upside down.

7. Yes. A $100 bill is worth more than a $1 bill (newer one).

8. Do not see because the next 72 hours will be midnight. Which you will not see the sunlight of course

9. The last piece of cloth will be cut in 7 days.

10. The answer is 5 minutes as well, because the more sewing machines are added, the more the shirt can be cut. Within the same time

11. Move the other rod the middle match will turn into a border.

12. When the balloon is blown by the wind the flag that is attached will not be waved to any direction.

13. "Are you still alive?"

14. decimal point

15. He sits on your own lap.

16. 1 + 17 - 3 = 9 + 6

17. Because seven ate nine.

18. 9 (6+4=10; minus the one you've taken off the shelf)

19. Number of cookies: a. Twelve b. Twelve

20. 3 (the grandfather is also a father and the father is also the son)

21. $18 ($4.50 per leg)

22. Zero, roosters do not lay eggs

23. A coin

24. 100 eggs, at one penny each

25. 5

26. 6

27. Zero

28. 4 (4x6=24)

29. Three mice, 30 : 1,5 = 20   60 : 20 = 3

30. Ten years from now, each of them will be ten years older so, 48+50=98

31. 3 days, the third day he starts at yard 2!!

Chapter 12 Easy Math Riddles Answers

1. They will end up with 335 fish.

2. James' dad is 42 years old.

3. Greg is 11 years old.

4. Tina picked 12 apples.

5. The Birchwood family has 27 girls.

6. Each person should get four toys

7. The next number in the pattern is 256. Each number in the sequence is multiplied by the number before it to get the next number.

8. Janet has $28 remaining.

9. Coach Ross should buy four basketballs.

10. A successful sale means the grocery store will sell at least nine cartons of milk.

11. Justin should give the cashier six quarters.

12. The answer is 12, so the number in the ones place is 2.

13. After three weeks, the chicken has laid 42 eggs.

14. The soda costs $4 and the burger costs $6.

15. There are 28 animals in the zoo. 16 are adults and 12 are babies.

16. After making his purchases, David has $8 left.

17. The missing number is 22. The numbers in the sequence increase by seven each time.

18. They spent 70 minutes, or an hour and 10 minutes, in the grocery store. Keep in mind that if the drive to the grocery store is 10 minutes, then the drive home takes an additional 10 minutes.

19. Since the change Leon is carrying only adds up to $1.70, he does not have enough money to buy the chips.

20. At the end of two weeks, Kyra will run seven miles.

21. The average number of pancakes eaten is three, eaten by Lisa.

22. I am thinking of the number 15.

23. John's sister is 16.

24. The ice cream man has five ice cream cones left.

25. The next number in the pattern is 243. Each number is being multiplied by 3 to get the next number.

26. Each question should take Jason four minutes.

27. The bat costs $20 and the glove costs $10.

28. The solution to the equation is 204, so the number that opens the lock is zero.

29. Clarissa is 11 years old. Her mother is 33.

30. Yes, Larry will finish his essay in time. At the pace of 120 words per day, Larry can write 600 words by Friday, which is more than enough for his essay.

31. I am thinking of the number 16.

32. Dahlia finished more monkey bars than Iris.

33. On Friday, Walt has $7 left. This is the $5 he saved on Tuesday plus the $2 he didn't spend on Thursday.

34. Yasmine finished all of her homework at 4:35 PM.

35. The missing number in the pattern is 8. Every number in the sequence gets divided by two to give the next number.

36. Calvin will finish building the rocket ship at 2:10 PM, which means he will have just enough time to finish it before soccer practice.

37. The popcorn costs $13 and the soda costs $8.

38. Jacob and Isabelle started shopping at 3:45 PM.

39. Trayvon is four years old.

40. There are 12 chickens in the coop.

41. It's 70. You're separating 30 by utilizing $\frac{1}{2}$, presently not by methods for two. Thirty separated through $\frac{1}{2}$ is a similar factor as increasing it by method for two that is 60. Additionally, 10 makes 70!

42. Meat. He takes a shot at the butcher store, so he gauges meat professionally

43. Seven. The enigma says everything except seven flee, which implies there are seven remaining who didn't.

44. Multiple times. On the third time, you'll get either a white or a blue sock to fit with one of the other two you've just snatched.

45. It may take fifty-one days. On the off chance that the scope of vegetation copies each day, a large portion of the grass may be finished the day sooner than, on the 51st day.

46. 888 +88 +8

47. Ashley is 22. Her mom is 22 years more seasoned, so when Ashley is 22, she's presently 50% of her mother's age.

Chapter 13 Intermediate Riddles Answers

1. The answer is 225, so the digit in the ones place is five. ()

2. Paul is 15 and his sister is 20. $\frac{3}{4}$ of 20 is 15, and Tommy and his

3. There are 86,400 seconds in a day.

4. The highest single digit prime number is seven, so the solution is

5. With $3, you can buy 72 eggs.

6. You can make six cups of lemonade per pitcher, so with three pitchers you can make 24 cups of lemonade.

7. With 5 $\frac{1}{2}$ waffles eaten, Riley wins the waffle eating contest.

8. At most, you will have to pull out a sock three times. Even if you are unlucky and you pull out two socks that don't match for your first two choices, the third sock will always match one of the ones you have already taken.

9. Trevor spends 100 minutes at practice altogether, which means he spends 50 minutes at baseball

practice and 25 minutes at lacrosse practice. The break between the two practices is the remaining time, which is 25 minutes

10. With these new measurements of time, there would be 4800 seconds in three hours.

11. Larissa has $8 after spending a third and $4 left after spending half of her remaining money. After she spends $2 on candy, she has just $2 left.

12. Each pizza slice should be split into thirds. This will produce 24 small slices of pizza. Everyone in the group of six friends can have four of the small slices of pizza.

13. 24 of the kids who buy lunch want plain milk and 48 want chocolate milk. This means there is enough of each type of milk for everyone to get what they want.

14. Melanie can buy three of the sweet candies with her dollar, which will give her the highest number of candies out of any combination. Every other combination of candies only allows her to buy two candies.

15. The result of the operations is the number 252.

16. The next number in the pattern is 12. What you do to get the next number in the pattern alternates between adding four and subtracting two. Add four to zero to get four, subtract two to get two, add four

again to get six, and continue until you reach the end of the pattern. Since you get eight by subtracting two from 10, the next step is to add four to eight to get the missing number.

17. Mr. Ace has 20 ice cream cones left at the end of the day. He sells a total of 10 cones before his delivery, which means after his delivery of 10 cones he is back to 25 cones. One fifth of 25 is five, so subtract five from 25 to get the remaining 20 ice cream cones.

18. Polly is allowed to eat no more than three cookies

19. Jonathan is 30 years old. The factors of 30 are one, two, three, five, six, 10, 15, and 30.

20. It will take Layton seven weeks to have enough money to buy the headphones. He is able to save $4 every week, so by the end of week seven he will have $28, which is a dollar more than he needs to make the purchase.

21. Dylan's lunch costs him $4.45, which means he has $0.55 left. He does not have enough money for the cookie.

22. If the film is $4.50, the camera is $28.00. The cost of both items together is $32.50.

23. Miya practiced for a total of 105 minutes. $\frac{1}{3}$ of an hour is 20 minutes, $\frac{1}{2}$ of an hour is 30 minutes, and $\frac{1}{4}$

of an hour is 15 minutes. ⅔ of an hour is 40 minutes. Adding all of Miya's practice time together using these values gives you 105 minutes

24. Kerrie sells 203 cups of lemonade in June, July, and August combined.

25. Julio still has $10 left after spending $10.

26. Nancy's tower is eight cards tall and Jaden's tower is 16 cards tall. This means Jaden's tower wins the competition.

27. Each student should get eight pretzels.

28. Natasha spends 15 minutes on her vocabulary homework. Five minutes are spent reviewing the words and 10 minutes are spent spelling them from memory.

29. The grocery store sold five times more watermelons on Friday than they did on Thursday.

30. Frankie and his friends have two and a half sandwiches.

31. You get 0.55 as your answer.

32. 20 percent of $23 is $4.60, so Diana's new total is $27.60.

33. $\frac{1}{2}$ is larger than ⅓, so you know that the aquarium has more clownfish than blue tangs even without knowing how many they have of each type of fish.

34. Each piece of cake should be cut into thirds. This will make 12 smaller slices of cake. Each person can have four of the smaller slices.

35. The missing time is 2:10 PM. You alternate adding 20 minutes and subtracting 10 minutes to get the next number in the pattern.

36. 32 people are now on the bus. There were 35 people on the bus after it made its first stop.

37. Edward will have two full bottles of apple juice. He will also have one extra bottle that is only ⅔ full.

38. Collin is 14 years old.

39. 7:30 PM on a 24-hour clock would be 19:30.

40. The guests want 14 hotdogs, 7 plain burgers, and 14 cheeseburgers. There are enough burgers and hotdogs for everyone, but two people who want cheese will have to have plain burgers.

Chapter 14 Moderate Math Riddles

1. Let the daughter's age be x; Imelda's age will be then x+24; in two years time; ()

2. X+2 = 1/2 (x+24+2); solve for x and Imelda's daughter's age will be 22.

3. The answer will be 0.

4. 13,212A.204. $56.25; 100-25% of 100 = $75 and a further 25% on this is 75 – 25% * 75 = 56.25

5. 44 years; total age of all the students is 22 * 21 = 462; total age including that of the teacher is 23 * 22 = 506; therefore, the age of the teacher is 506 – 462 = 44 years.

6. 8 pieces; cut two ways diagonally in the usual way, and then, cut horizontally through the middle of the cake.

7. Zero; before 24 days is one day.

8. 16 years; let Vincent's and Sean's ages six years ago be 6x and 5x; after 4 years, their ratios will create an equation like: 11(5x+10) = 10 (6x + 10); solve for x and you will get 2; So the present age of Sean is 5*2 + 6 = 16

9. 15 years; Sharon's present age is 26-6 = 20; let Sean's present age be x; the ratio equation will be 20/x = 4/3 solve for x and you will get 15 years.

10. 40 years; let his mother's age be x, then John's age is 2/5x; the equation formed is: X+8 = 2 (2/5x + 8) solve for x to get his mother's current age.

11. 60 years; let the nephew's age be x, then the brother's age is 2x, the sister's age is 4x, and the father's age is 12x which totals to 19x; the only number below 100 that fits all the requirements is 95; so, 19x = 95; x = 5; so the father's age = 12 * 5 = 60 years.

12. 6 years; Sharon's father's age 4 years later (when her sister was born) would have been 42; her mother's age at that time is already known to be 36; so the difference in their ages is 42 -36 = 6 years.

13. Yes, it does make sense to switch because the chances of winning has increased from 1/3 to 2/3.

14. The last sum-day of the 21st century will be 31 December 2043 (31 + 12 = 43); all the big numbers are used up and, therefore, there will be no more sum-days after this in the 21st century.

15. 365 days; this is easy to see because every day (in a non-leap year) is a sum-day for any one year in a century; for example; November 26 will be the sum-

day for 2037; similarly, January 26 will be the sum-day for 2028, and so forth. The only day which will not be a sum-day is February 29 because 2 + 29 = 31; however, 31 is not a leap year.

16. Penny will again win the race because in the first race when Jenny reached 95 m, Penny had run 100m. In the second race, both the girls will reach the 95 m point at the same time (100-95). Now, since Penny is faster than Jenny, she will complete the balance 5 m before Jenny.

17. 4 (in a set of quadruplets) + 2 (twins) + 3 (triplets) = 9

18. E= 1/4L, 20= T, 20= L, E= 1/4 x 20, E= 5, Y= 1/4 x 20, and Y= 5; (E –eating, Y – yawning, T – thinking, and L – laughing)

19. When they meet, they will be at the same distance from New Jersey.

20. First, he takes the rabbit and leaves the carrots and the fox behind. He then comes back, takes the sack of carrots, leaves it on the destination back and brings back the rabbit. Now, he takes the fox and leaves the rabbit in the other bank. He then returns third time to ferry the rabbit again.

21. Each brother got (75+45)/3 = 40 sacks. Each sack cost $1400/40 = $35. Adam got (45-40)*$35 = $175 and David got (75-40)*$35 = #1225

22. 5 The equations represent the number of letters in the name of each number.

23. 7th jump will take him to 15 feet, which will let him out of the well.

24. 12 years; let his age be x, the equation is x = 2 = 2(x-5)

25. 8 children; there is only one sister.

26. 10 (5 on each side).

27. Both ends of the chain are on the same nail. If 10 feet of chain has to dip down 5-feet, then this is the only explanation.

28. By thinking out of the box; SIX - 9(IX) = S, 9 (IX) - 10 (X) = I, 40 (XL) - 50 (L) = X; SIX!

29. He is 50 years old.

30. Every number in this sequence is what comes between two successive prime numbers starting from 3 and 5. So, the next in series is 150 (because it comes between the next pair of prime numbers; 149 and 151.

31. 24 and 42

32. Volume = π(radius)2*depth = pizza!

33. 2.1 pounds

34. David – 73, his daughter – 37

35. 56; start with 88 applicants because 12 have no prior experience, and then take it forward.

36. 34 hens and 17 sheep

37. 2357947691; 111, 113, 115, 117, 119

38. Apple is 52 cents, pear is 83 cents, banana is 57 cents.

39. $9 * 8 - 7 + 6 * 5 - 4 = 91$

40. 56 chickens, 41 geese, and 3 cows

41. The value of each barrel is 120 francs and the duty payable is 10 francs per barrel

42. One thousand

43. The number is 7; let it be x and form equations with the word problems and solve for x

44. $4991: $[6435+6927+6855+7230+6562 + x]/6 = 6500$; solve for x

45. 60 and 6, 51 and 15, and 24 and 42

46. $4000; let the income of Mr. Adam, Mr. Bobby, and Mr. Crew be x, y, and z. Form the three equations with the given data and solve for the unknown.

47.78; these are multiples of 13 with their digits reversed

48.67 kg; my idea is $65 < x < 72$; like this create inequalities for the others and you will find a number that fits all guesses.

Chapter 15 Medium Riddles Answers

1. The next number is $\frac{1}{4}$. Divide the previous number in the sequence by two to get the new number. ()

2. 80 out of the 240 available seats are filled, which is $\frac{1}{3}$ of the auditorium's seats.

3. You end up with the number 141.5.

4. Five eggs remain in the nest at the end of the first week. The chicken lays 15 eggs in a week, which leaves 10 eggs for the farmer to take.

5. At the end of five days, the garden will contain 1024 flowers.

6. I am thinking of the number 55.

7. Three out of the four different coat patterns include brown, so the chances of the farmer choosing one of those horses is $\frac{3}{4}$.

8. Zoo two has 32 flamingos and zoo three has 80 flamingos.

9. The total number of flowers on all four floats is 2,748.

10. In 40 minutes, the cheetah can run about 47 miles.

11. The penguins walk 84 miles in three weeks.

12. One ton equals 2000 pounds.

13. Ashley makes a total of $28.50 at the fundraiser. $12 comes from brownies, $12 comes from cookies, and $4.50 comes from cake pops.

14. Damian's family started dinner at 4:55 PM.

15. The restaurant sold 38 drinks, 114 celery sticks, and 190 chicken wings.

16. Yes, there are enough drinks for everyone to get what they want. 20 kids want each type of drink and all of the drinks have more than 20 bottles available.

17. The next number is 900. The pattern alternates between doubling the previous number and subtracting 50, so you should double 450 to get the next number.

18. The neighborhood now contains 46 families.

19. It takes Greg 19 days to finish all of his candy. The original 30 pieces takes him 15 days to eat and the additional eight pieces takes him another four days.

20. Selina's grandmother is 82 years old.

21. To make 24 cupcakes, you should use three cups of sugar.

22. You will need four containers. Three cups of rice weighs about 1.5 pounds, which is $\frac{1}{4}$ of six pounds.

23. There are 36 roses in total, which means each rose cost $1.50.

24. The candle burns for 140 minutes, or two hours and 20 minutes.

25. Annalise sent 12 messages on Monday, 18 on Tuesday, six on Wednesday, zero on Thursday, and 24 on Friday.

26. Beth spent 34.5 hours ice skating, which is 11.5 more hours than Henry.

27. There are 18 baskets of oranges.

28. Linda made a total of $214.50. She made $97.50 in the first week and $117 in the second week.

29. Mr. Hopper's daughter is 14 years old.

30. Jackie should spend no more than $14 on each friend's gift. Spending more than that may mean she runs out of money and has to buy someone a less expensive present.

Chapter 16 Hard Level Riddles Answers

1. Between 3 and 4 PM, the service center received 600 + (60/100 * 600) = 960 calls. Therefore, the number of calls per minute between 3 and 4 is 960/60 = 16 calls ()

2. The chances are 50% irrespective of what happened in the previous toss.

3. 61; get each number in the sequence by doubling the previous number and adding three to it; the last number is 29*2 + 3

4. 63; each number is obtained by cubing 1, 2, 3, 4, and then subtracting 1 from it.

5. 35; The present ages of Pat and Quentin will be 3x and 4x; So, ten years ago, the equation that represents the relations between their ages is: $3x - 10 = \frac{1}{2}(4x-10)$; solve for x and the answer is 5; Pat's age is 15 and Quentin's age is 20. So the total is 15 + 20 = 35.

6. 9 books are on the shelf

7. Let the age of the youngest child be x, then the other 5 children's age will be x+3, x+6, x+9, x+12. The

equations is x + x+3 + x+6 + x+9 + x+12 = 50; solve for x and the youngest child's age is 4 years.

8. Light both the ends of the first rope and only one end of the second rope. In half an hour, the first rope will burn down completely while the second rope will be half burned. At this point, light the unlit end of the second rope too. In 15 minutes, the second rope will burn down completely. So, the total time taken in 30 + 15 = 45 minutes.

9. 14 years; let the son be x years now; then, 38-x = x; solve this and you get x as 19 which is the present age of the son; therefore, five years ago, he would have been 14 years old.

10. Put 3 balls on each side of the weight. If the scales are balanced, then the one that is not weighed is the lightest one. If one of these have the lighter ball, then that side will be tilted up. Take that set of three balls and place one on each scale. Again, if they are even, the one from this three which was not measured is the light ball. Else, the side of the scale tilted up is the light one.

11. He has to travel 110 km so that the mileage meter reads 73037.

12. 3021

13. 16 days; for this, we'll work backward (keep in mind he doubles his task every day) On day 18; 100% of his task was done. On day 15; 50% of his task was done. On day 16, 25% of the task was done.

14. 24 $\frac{1}{2}$ years; let Kate's age be 7x and Beck's age be 9x. 9x – 7x = 7; solve for x and you will get 3.5; Kate's age is 7*3.5 = 24 $\frac{1}{2}$ years old.

15. 22 toffees; first, you buy 15 toffees and eat them up, you are left with 15 wrappers that will get you 5 more toffees, after eating all the 5 toffees, get one more toffee by returning three wrappers, and finally give your last 3 wrappers and get one more.

16. 40 years

17. You need to cut only one 1/7th and one 2/7th. Day 1: Cut at the 1/7th place and give him his first payment. Day 2: Cut 2/7th and give him the payment after taking back the first 1/7th. Day 3: Give him the 1/7th you took from him on Day 2. Day 4: Give him the balance of the bar, which is 4/7ths, and take back the 2/7th and the 1/7th. Day 5: Give him the 1/7th. Day 6: Give him the 2/7th and take back the 1/7th. Day 7: Give him the 1/7th.

18. 29 rungs

19. $2300; solve the three equations that can be formed with the information.

20. 6 * 6 + 66 / 6 + 66 = 113

21. 112,589,991,000 m! The power of compounding!

22. 3 cents

23. Daisy costs $0.50 each and tulip costs $1

24. 100; work backward and you will have the answer in a jiffy.

25. Head = 3 inches, Tail = 3 inches and the middle part = 9 inches

26. 42; the LCM of 2, 3, and 7

27. 58

28. 3 brothers and 4 sisters

29. 8 pounds

30. If it is 11 am and I add 2 hours, then I get 1 pm.

31. 19 numbers can be greater than 0.

32. 43 – Explanation: After 6 all numbers divisible by 3 can be ordered (because they can all be expressed as a sum of 6's and 9's). After 26, all numbers divisible by three when subtracted by 20 can be obtained. After 46, all numbers divisible by three when subtracted by 40 can be obtained. After 46, all numbers fit into one of these 3 categories, so all numbers can be obtained. 43 is the last number that

doesn't fall into one of these categories ($44 = 20 + 6 * 4$, $45 = 6 * 6 + 9$).

33. $7.98; Calculate the total amount of fuel he bought each year and then arrive at the answer.

34. $9 + 8 + 7 + 6 + 5 + 4 + 3 + 2 + 1 = 90$

35. 285; a 30-day month will have 4 full weeks and the two days will be a Sunday and a Monday; use this information and the averages given to arrive at the answer.

36. 789; get every number by doubling the previous number and then either adding or subtracting 1 alternately.

37. 40 students

38. 50 pounds of water have evaporated.

39. 52; There are two series here; figure out the first one by adding 8 to the previous number and the next one by adding 15 to the previous number.

40. 31 kg; $A + B + C = 45$; $A + B = 40$; and $B + C = 43$; there are three equations and three unknowns which is easy to solve.

41. 5 mph; Total distance is 60 miles; time taken is $4\frac{1}{2}$ hours; speed downstream is $15 + x$ (speed of the stream); and speed upstream is $15 - x$; now it will be easy to calculate.

42. Start both the hourglasses; flip the 11-minute hourglass when it completes its first round; now when the 13 minutes is done, flip the 11-minute hourglass back because the reverse would be 2 minutes.

43. -6; there are two series; get one by adding 4 and the other by subtracting 3.

44. 33 years

45. 245 m; the distance traveled at 45 mph in 30 seconds is 130 + length of the bridge, use the given data and get your answer.

46. $1.19; one half dollar, one quarter, 4 dimes, and four pennies.

47. Initially, 20 people got $6 each; then 15 (20-15) would have gotten $8; now, with 24 people each would have gotten $5.

48. 196; the rest are all in the following pattern: 13, 23, 33, 43, 53...

49. 33+51+72=81

50. 833 apples; first you make three trips of 333 with 1000 apples each. You will have 2001 apples and 667 miles still to cover. Next, you make 2 trips of 500 miles at the end of which you will have 1000 and 167 miles more to cover. (Here you will have to leave behind that one lone apple); the last trip of 167 miles

with 1000 apples will use up 167 apples for duty, and you will be left with 833 apples for the market.

Chapter 17 Challenging Math Riddles Answers

1. The exhibit should be 13 feet long by 11 feet wide. ()

2. You can buy four dozen eggs, or 48 eggs. You will have $0.04 left.

3. The perimeter of the playground is 44 feet.

4. Mikayla's mom got $1 \frac{3}{4}$ pounds of cold cuts, or 1.75 pounds.

5. There are 11,063 deer altogether.

6. Hamster B weighs four pounds and hamster C weighs six pounds.

7. There are 27 cats with either patches or stripes.

8. The fish tank would cost them $480, so they do not have enough money in the budget for a tank of this size.

9. The missing number is 21.8. Each number in the pattern is multiplied by 0.2 to get the next number.

10. The picture frame's area is 16.1 square inches.

11. You end up with the number 471.48.

12. The remaining 9/12 of the bottle is white grape juice, which is simplified to $\frac{3}{4}$ of the bottle.

13. The height of the triangle is 13 feet.

14. The shorter tree is 30.125 feet tall and the taller tree is 34.125 feet tall.

15. The next number is 8,192. You get the next number by multiplying the two previous numbers together.

16. Three times nine is 27. Then subtract seven to get 20.

17. Terry can have five cookies, as this is the largest number that fits all of the criteria his mother gave

18. Kennedy ran 4,620 feet in 4.5 minutes and 3,960 feet in 3.75 minutes. This is equal to about 1,027 feet in a minute on Tuesday and 1,056 feet in a minute on Wednesday, meaning he ran faster on Wednesday.

19. The area of the sheep pen is 4056 square feet.

20. Yes, Owen has enough money to buy the cards. The sales tax on the cards is $0.61, making the total cost of the cards $9.36, which is less than $10.

21. $\frac{1}{3}$ of $\frac{1}{4}$ is 1/12, so James ate 1/12 of the whole birthday cake.

22. 54 houses need their lawns mowed, which will take the lawn care company 13 $\frac{1}{2}$ hours.

23. Trisha paid $81.67 every month.

24. Snakes with at least some black scales make up 35 percent of the snakes in the forest. This is about 206 snakes.

25. You would have 12 full containers and one container $\frac{4}{5}$ full.

26. You should play. Red and yellow make up 7/13 of the spinner sections, which is over half.

27. Mount Everest is 778 feet taller than K2.

28. $\frac{2}{3}$ is larger than $\frac{1}{2}$ and $\frac{3}{5}$, so Gina eats the most pizza.

29. The house has a width of 25 feet and a length of 33 feet.

30. 100 cookies would be 6.25 batches, so you would need about 4.7 cups of sugar.

31. The final batch is done at 1:22 PM. Remember that even though the last batch only contains a quarter of the usual number of cookies, it has to bake for the same amount of time.

32. The box can hold an additional one pound and five ounces. The total weight already in the box is 21 pounds and nine ounces.

33. Start by multiplying three times six, then subtract four. Finally, multiply by five.

34. One box weighs 40 ounces and the other weighs 56 ounces. Together they weigh 96 ounces.

35. 0.25 cups, or $\frac{1}{4}$ cup of chicken stock goes into each bowl.

36. The store gave out 30 $\frac{3}{4}$, or 30.75 bottles of juice. 246 samples is 984 ounces of juice, which can be converted to 123 cups and finally 30.75 bottles.

37. The perimeter of the fence is 26.25 feet. The first side is seven feet, the second is 10.5 feet, and the third is 8.75 feet.

38. The box of cupcakes weighs 9/13 pounds.

39. There are 34 more koalas than kangaroos, so the koala exhibit must be 136 square feet larger than the kangaroo exhibit. This means the area of the koala exhibit is 218 square feet.

40. The apple weighs 5.25 ounces, the banana weighs 4.50 ounces, and the orange weighs 4.75 ounces.

Chapter 18 For Fun Answer

1. Red – 36, Green – 8 and Blue – 15 ()

2. The lion will get $16; $4 for each leg

3. Gerry bought 6 oranges, ate 2 (1/3) on the first day, and another 2 ($\frac{1}{2}$ of the remaining 4) on the second day.

4. 7; Let the number be x and form the equation using the clues as follows: ((47 + x)*3)/2 = 81. Solve for x and get the answer.

5. 41 years ago; Sarah was 39, and Sandra was 13.

6. Frances is 13 and her brother is 5; Here is a way to solve it: let Frances' brother's age be x, then her age is x + 8; three years hence, the equation will be: x+8+3 = 2(x+3); solve for x and you will get Frances' brother's age as 5.

7. Tilt the glass slowly and gently until the water reaches the rim of the glass. Now, if the water in the bottom half is in perfect alignment with the bottom rim, then the glass is exactly half-full.

8. This is a clock and you need to add two hours to 11 o'clock in the morning to get one o'clock in the evening.

9. Let Peter's present age be x; his father's age is 4x; after 8 years, the equation will be: $4x + 8 = 5/2 (x + 8)$; solve for x and you will get 8. So Peter is 8 and his father is 36

10. It never will be because when the water rises, the ship and the ladder over its side will rise too.

11. Let Sam and Peter's age be 5x and 4x. Three years from now, the age equation will be $5x + 3 / 4x + x = 11 / 9$ solve for x and then replace in 5x and 4x and you will get their ages as 30 and 24

12. The minute hand is exactly at 3 and the hour hand is exactly quarter way between 3 and 4. Each hour has 30 degrees between them. So, the hour hand is at $30/4 = 7 \frac{1}{2}$ degrees away from three, which is where the minute hand is. Therefore, the angle between the hour and minute hands is 7.5 degrees at 3:15.

13. 5 years; Let Adam's present age be x; then his father's age is 6x; after ten years, Adam's father's age will be $6x + 10$ which is twice that of what Sharon will be; therefore Sharon's age 10 years hence will be $\frac{1}{2} * (6x +10)$; Sharon is now 10 years old, because she celebrated her 8th birthday 2 years ago. So, 10 years

hence, she will be 20 years; putting everything together $\frac{1}{2}$ *(6x + 10) = 20; solve for x and you will get 5 years.

14. Just 2 because every time you give half of what you are carrying, they will return 1 and so at the end of the journey, you will have the 2 cakes you carried for your grandmother.

15. His average speed is 3 mph. He takes one hour to climb up and takes 20 minutes? to climb down. So, his total time is 1 hour 20 minutes to complete 4 miles. That gives you an average speed of 3 mph.

16. You just need to cut the gold bar twice; cut the gold bar into 1 piece of 1 unit and 2 pieces of 2 units (1/5th is one unit); one day one, you give him 1 unit; one day 2, you give him one of the 2-unit pieces and take back the one-unit piece; on day three, give him the one-unit piece again; one day four; take back the one-unit piece and give him the remaining 2-unit piece, and on day five, give him the one-unit piece.

17. Son – 20 years; let the present age of the son be x; therefore, father's age is 60 – x; Six years ago, the equation between their ages is: (60 – x) – 6 = 5 (x – 6); solve for x and you will get 14 years and so, 6 six years hence, he will be 20 years.

18. The four page numbers are 19, 20, 45, and 46; page # 46 will be on the other side of 45; the pages are arranged in pairs in such a way that one pair totals to 64, and the other pair totals to 66; therefore, the page number opposite 45 will be 64-45 = 19 and the page number opposite 46 will be 44-46 = 20.

19. 1 mph; David was canoeing at a constant speed in relation to the river velocity. He took a total of 8 hours to complete 24 miles. When he lost his hat, David had paddled for two hours. To meet David on his return journey at the start of the journey, the hat would have had to travel downstream for six hours because David paddled for 18 miles more (or 6 hours more) to be at that point. Therefore, it took the hat six hours to travel 6 miles which is 1 mph.

20. 16, 27, 46; let their current ages be $4x$, $7x$, and $9x$; so the equation formed will be $(4x - 8) + (7x-8) + (9x - 8) = 56$; solve for x to get 4 and use that to get the present ages.

21. 5040 different ways; 7*6 + 6*5 + 5*4 + 4*3 + 3*2 + 2*1; the first person has 7 different choices, the second person has 6 different choices, and so forth.

22. No, it is not possible to get the answer because the data is insufficient.

23. Label the bottles 1, 2, 3, 4, and 5; take 1 pill from the first bottle, 2 pills from bottle 2, 3 pills from bottle 3, 4 from bottle 4, and 5 from bottle 5; put all of the 15 pills on the weighing scale; if the weight is 149 gm, then the first bottle is contaminated, if the weight is 148 the second bottle is contaminated, if the weight is 147 then the third bottle is contaminated, if the weight is 146, the fourth bottle is the problem, and if the weight is 145, the fifth bottle is the problem.

24. 19.2 m

25. 21104; get the first set of digits by multiplying the two numbers; get the second set by adding the two numbers and get the last set of digits by subtracting the two numbers.

26. 150 miles; at the speed of 30 mph, I was using $1\frac{1}{2}$ gallons of petrol per hour and also losing $\frac{1}{2}$ gallon because of the leak. Therefore, every hour 2 gallons of petrol were being consumed. The total time traveled is 10 gallons / 2 gallons which is 5 hours. The distance traveled is 30 mph * 5 = 150 miles.

27. 84 years; the equation is as follows: let his age be x; $x/6 + x/12 + x/7 + 5 + x/2 + 4 = x$; solve for x

28. 30 campers; work like this. If there were 6 people, then there would have been 6 bowls of soup, 3 spaghetti bowls, and 2 salad bowls.

29. 49 steps

30. 7:3

31. 27

32. Simply bring all the four corners of the square to the center. The square's thickness will be doubled and the area will be halved.

33. The price of the fourth item is $0.50.

34. Square root of [(0.2)-2]

35. 2 minutes is the shortest interval; between 9:59 and 10:01

36. 4, 3, 8 / 9, 5, 1 / 2, 7, 6

37. 22 children because at half of the circle there are 11 (18-7).

38. Gerry 24 and Carl 20

39. 7, 4, 6, 5, and 8

40. He sold 14 smoothies at $2; 14 @ $2 + 18 @ $3 for 4 gave him $52.

Chapter 19 More Math Riddles Answer

1. Businessmen have profit from selling horses 2 times, including 20 baht, first sales, profit 10 baht, second sales, profit 10 baht, a total of 20 baht ()

2. The bottom floor, because no matter which floor Must always press the elevator to the bottom floor

3. If the light is lit at the end of a rope and burns out in 1 hour, so you can light the fire at both ends. The rope will burn out within 30 minutes. 2 sides and the end of the second rope only one side and after the first rope burns out (30 minutes), start the fire at the end of the remaining second rope, which will burn out within 15 minutes, including 2 lines for 45 minutes.

4. Pencil placed on the wall You can't jump over.

5. Throwing tennis balls up to the sky and it will float back to you. How to solve the problem of stolen shoes Nike set up another factory. Then let both factories produce separate left and right shoes 7 Look at the watch because the number 2 means 10 minutes.

6. The buffalo that can't conceive Because it is a male buffalo

7. A 17-year-old brother and a younger brother, 7 years old, two years ago, they were 15 years old and 5 years in the next three years. They will be 20 years and 10 years, respectively.

8. Instead of the number of patients is x. The number of bites in 1 week is 7x. The number of bite patients 2 times per person is 2x. Doctor was bitten 100 times, translated into equation equals $7x-2x = 100$, so $x = 20$. The answer is the number of patients equal to 20.

9. The patient splits 1 chain into 3 rings and then connects with the remaining 4 lines.

10. The suspect has 2 people. The first is the chef. Who said that he was making breakfast even though it was evening and the butler who is saying that he talks to the workers But no other worker in the house anymore?

11. Detective Stevens follows a travel company about booking plane tickets to travel to the mountains. And found that Mr. Clyde had booked 2 air tickets but booked only one ticket back.

12. If assuming that the side that is standing on side A and the other side is B side, first he must take the wolf to side B, then return to pick up the first sheep on the side A to take to the side B and bring the wolf Take it back to the side of A again, then leave the wolf on the side A to bring the second sheep to the side B, then return to pick up the wolf at side A for the final round.

13. The police didn't tell the husband that Where is the scene? But the husband can travel right

14. He must take 7 days due to the last 2 feet of fabric. He doesn't need to cut. Jane's poison on a single knife and when slicing half the steak She picked up the steak piece that was poisoned by her husband to eat.

15. Choose the second bloom because if the lion doesn't eat anything for 3 years, it won't survive.

16. The upper left prisoner Try to dye your own dress to be green. In order to harmonize with the supervisor but was arrested before

17. Clark didn't know that his wife had been shot. He heard from the housekeeper that there was only a disaster. How did he know that his wife was shot?

18. Yes, Larry will finish his essay in time. At the pace of 120 words per day, Larry can write 600 words by Friday, which is more than enough for his essay.

19. I am thinking of the number 16.

20. Dahlia finished more monkey bars than Iris.

21. On Friday, Walt has $7 left. This is the $5 he saved on Tuesday plus the $2 he didn't spend on Thursday.

22. Yasmine finished all of her homework at 4:35 PM

23. The missing number in the pattern is 8. Every number in the

24. sequence gets divided by two to give the next number.

25. Calvin will finish building the rocket ship at 2:10 PM, which means he will have just enough time to finish it before soccer practice.

26. The popcorn costs $13 and the soda costs $8.

27. Jacob and Isabelle started shopping at 3:45 PM.

28. Trayvon is four years old.

29. There are 12 chickens in the coop.

30. Jackie should read 25 pages for each of the five days.

31. You end up with the number 11.

32. There are nine rain jackets hanging up.

33. The aquarium will have 25 sharks. 10 of the sharks are adults and 15 are babies.

34. The next number in the pattern is 36.

35. 540 seconds is equivalent to nine minutes, so Jared ran the mile a minute faster than Sarah.

36. Christina scores 11 points for her team during the game.

37. Mrs. Driscoll could assign worksheets one and two. She could also assign worksheets one and three. Assigning worksheets two and three, or assigning all three worksheets, would meet or exceed the 30-minute time limit.

38. I am thinking of the two-digit number 19. A two-digit number's first number cannot be 0, so it must be 1. Any number 10 or larger is more than one digit, so the second digit must be nine.

Chapter 20 Bonus Riddle Answers

1. Yes, if he was born on 1896, February 29; the next leap year will be eight years later.   ()

2. She could get the highest possible average if she got 0 in one of her tests; then her new average will be 68*9/8 = 76.5

3. Three; you will get 2 of one color or 3 of the same color.

4. 4 slices

5. 2 + 2/2

6. Rhombus

7. 12,111

8. 1, 2, and 3

9. 4952

10. 2999 + 3000 + 3001

11. 128 inches; head – 4 inches, body - 96 inches, tail - 28 inches

12. 60 sets; 5 * 4 * 3

13. -40 = -40; the equations represent the relation between Celsius and Fahrenheit temperatures.

14. A sphere

15. It is a sequence that is obtained by adding 1 to every digit in the value of π (3.1415926535...)

16. 2.828 cm; the four corners of the square touch the circle and the diagonal is its diameter; use the Pythagoras theorem to find the answer.

17. Let the age of Cat be x; then Bobby's age will be 2x and Andrea will be 2x + 2; X + 2x + 2x + 2 = 27; solve for x which will be 5, Bobby's age is 2x = 10 years old.

18. 60 sandwiches

19. 4 years ago

20. 18 minutes

21. $200; let x be the original amount; form the required equation based on the given information and solve for x

22. He fills the 9-cup jug and the 4-cup jug with water. He then transfers water from the 9-cup to the 6-cup jug leaving behind 3 cups. The filled 4-cup jug and the 3 cups in the 9-cup jug will give Rupert the required 7 cups of water.

23. 583*385

24. Michael will pay $12.50 and his friend will pay $7.50.

25. 12345679; 12345679 * 9 = 111111111, 12345679 * 18 = 222222222, 12345679 * 27 = 333333333, and so forth

26. 100 oranges

27. She needs to get 5 stars on three assignments so that the total stars will be 5*3 + 1 = 16; so, the average will be 16/4 = 4

28. 39 years ago, the oldest parent's (dad) age is between 39 and 41 which is 40 years; the game came about one year before my dad was born.

29. 19%; 187/981 where 981 is the total number of students

30. 25000 ml; no, the answer is not 32000 ml because superstitious people consider it bad luck to drink to their own toast.

31. Susan is 4 and Katherine is 5.

32. 54 feet; 1/2 + 1/3 = 5/6 is inside the lake and the balance 1/6, which is 9 ft, is outside the lake; if 1/6th is 9 ft, the total length of the pole is 54 feet.

33. The correct time is between 5 min and $5 \frac{1}{2}$ minutes past 2 PM.

34. 146097; 365 * 400 + 97 leap days

Math Riddles for Smart Kids

35. 90 degrees; you want to increase the speed by 10 mph which translates to turning the knob 1/4th of its full turn; $\frac{1}{4}$ of 360 degrees is 90.

36. 3; 3 + 1.5 = 4.5 and 3 * 1.5 = 4.5

37. Janet is 40 years, and Andrew is 30 years.

38. 2519

39. 9 minutes

40. 3

41. $100

42. 11 cartons; 7 large boxes (7*8 boxes) + 4 small boxes (4*10) = 96 cartons

43. She will never complete it because at each jump, she will be adding lesser and lesser distances.

44. 6.25

45. 20 teachers were sharing a bill totaling to $600

46. Each puzzle takes 6 minutes to solve. The 60 puzzles will take 360 minutes or 6 hours to be solved.

Finally, if you found this book useful in any way, a review on Amazon is always appreciated! CLICK HERE

Math Riddles for Smart Kids

Conclusion

Now that you and your child have completed the above riddles, you can enjoy the benefits that come from improved math skills and increased family time. Learning can be just as much of a bonding experience as play time. Combining learning and play together allows you child to develop their math, reasoning, and critical thinking skills in a way that supports a successful future.

You can expect to see a fair number of results from going through even a few riddles with your child. The first and most apparent benefit is to your child's math skills, which should see significant improvement with practice of arithmetic and logical thinking skills. You may even notice an increased desire for learning now that your child knows that math, and therefore other subjects, can be fun even when it is challenging. Solving these puzzles together also supports the development of a more close-knit family that tackles problems together and whose members rely on each other when they are presented with challenges.

These benefits are not limited to math riddles, nor are they limited to the contents. You can continue to apply them in your child's life by encouraging your child to ask for help when they are struggling, whether it is with a tricky math question or a difficult question they have encountered in their lives. Always be available and willing to help guide your child to the right answers, no matter the subject, and you will establish a close bond with your child that will help support them in all of their future endeavors.

That was fun, wasn't it? We hope you've had a good time with your little one or your dear friend, as you've gone through this with them. It is good practice, and you can use this at different points to the concepts that have been taught throughout the riddles. As you can see, riddles can be some of the most fulfilling and enjoyable word games to play with your loved ones. They will quickly see the value of solving riddles and find joy in the word puzzles that they are able to decode. It is not always easy to solve these puzzles, but once your child does solve them, they'll see the value in them.

Solving riddles is a great way to prepare your young one(s) for real life. It is not just a puzzle that picks at your brain and enables you to have a good time with words. Instead, it is something that leads you to become a better thinker in every respect. Your child will not only use these word puzzles to enjoy their young lives; he or she will also do much better in school and earn the best grades because of them. Also, your child will feel more confident in expressing his or her opinion out loud. Many children are shy and not comfortable sharing their thoughts with others. By getting your child to solve riddles, you will enable them to build the confidence that they need to interact with children their age and give them opportunities to be competitive in a friendly way.

Riddles are a great way for adults to explain to children how the answers to certain riddles come about. These riddles can easily be solved by most adults, in fact. When you work with your child to solve a riddle, you open up bonding opportunities with your children and your family as a whole. Solve these riddles with your family around the kitchen table after dinner and the room will surely be filled with joy and excitement.